GETTING IT DONE

The Best Kept Secrets
for Success in Business and Life

GETTING IT DONE

The Best Kept Secrets
for Success in Business and Life

———————— ◊ ————————

JOHN M. CAPOZZI

JMC Publishing Services
125 Brett Lane
Fairfield, CT 06824
(203) 255-8776

Published in the United States by
JMC Publishing Services
125 Brett Lane
Fairfield, Connecticut 06824
(203) 255-8776

Library of Congress Cataloging-in-Publication Data

Getting It Done:
The Best Kept Secrets for Success in Business and Life
By John M. Capozzi

First Edition

p.   cm.
ISBN 0-9656410-8-2
1. Business & Economics

Printed in the United States of America

100% of the author's royalties
from this book will be given
to educational scholarships
for children.

Other Books By John M. Capozzi:

**Why Climb the Corporate Ladder
When You Can Take the Elevator?**
500 Secrets for Success in Business and Life

**If You Want the Rainbow ...
You Gotta Put Up with the Rain!**
500 Secrets for Success in Business and Life

**A Spirit of Greatness:
Stories from the Employees of American Airlines**

Get A Grip!
(In association with Golf Digest)

**A Spirit of Golf:
Stories from Those Who Love the Game**
(In association with The PGA of America)

INTRODUCTION

For almost 30 years I have personally written or collected business maxims as a hobby. Several in my collection were coined by famous successful people, others by regular folks, and unfortunately, the source of many is unknown.

Several years ago, I was approached by a literary agent who wanted to write about my successful business career, specifically, about my 13 corporate promotions in 13 years. He suggested I write a "How To" book for anyone trying to get ahead in corporate life. Rather than write a traditional "How To" book, which had already been done so many times by so many people, I opted to capture my business philosophy through a collection of business maxims. I chose the title *Why Climb the Corporate Ladder When You Can Take the Elevator?* for my first book. A year later, I wrote a second book called, *If You Want the Rainbow You Gotta Put Up with the Rain!* as an extension of my first book.

This book, *Getting It Done*, contains some of the best maxims from both my first and second books along with some new stories. Most are fun and insightful. I am particularly pleased that based upon my own business experiences, I was able to personally create several hundred of the maxims contained in this book.

I chose the title "Getting It Done" after considering dozens of others for a very simple reason: it is the key to success in both business and life.

It really doesn't matter what you do for a living, or what your title is … CEO, manager, secretary, or mailroom clerk. If you want to get ahead, you must "get the job done" correctly and on time.

No matter what your job description says you do, if you simply do it well, you will have a job. If you do it better than anyone else, you will get promoted.

I have started over 20 companies that have never failed. I have helped at least a dozen of my employees become millionaires and I have made a lot of money for my family.

In addition, I continue to raise money and give my time and a portion of my personal proceeds toward the education of children, in particular, to children who are at risk. Our children are the future of our business community.

I totally believe that if anyone in business for themselves, or who works for a corporation, follows the wisdom of the maxims collected in this book, their odds for success will be far greater.

I have had a great deal of success in my business career and many people have told me how "lucky" I have been. But success in business is not about luck, it is about hard work and careful planning. I do not believe in the success theory of "being in the right place at the right time." Tireless persistence and creativity have put me in a position to find the opportunities I could easily have missed had I been at the beach or on the golf course.

My theory of the combination of tireless persistence and creativity began when I was ten years old and I started selling soda at a construction site across from my home. When I arrived with my wagon and cooler full of soda after school every day, the entire job would come to a halt when a worker yelled, "The soda kid's here!" I sold so much soda that my folks had to buy another refrigerator to keep in the garage for my inventory.

Throughout high school I shoveled snow every winter, worked in construction every summer, set bowling pins at a local YMCA in the evenings, and somehow found time to be active in sports and get my homework done. My college life wasn't any easier.

I attended college on Tuesday, Wednesday and Thursday from 9:00 a.m. to 10:00 p.m. in New York City. Going to both day school and night school allowed me to carry a full academic program and still hold down a variety of jobs every Friday, Saturday, Sunday, and Monday to cover costs. I think it all worked because I always enjoyed what I did.

One of my first college jobs was as a locker boy at an affluent men's health club directly across the street from the college I attended. Members identified themselves at my window and I retrieved a small wire basket with their sneakers and gym clothing. There were several other college students who worked this job between classes. It was a great job that allowed us to get paid for doing homework when the work was slow.

One day, a customer came to play squash, but his partner cancelled. He asked me if I would "hit" with him so that his court time wasn't a total loss. Having grown up in the New York area, my athletic skills at that moment consisted of knowing how to play stickball, how to fight, and how to run from all sorts of trouble. Squash was not in my repertoire. But, since I've never been one to turn down an offer without at least exploring it a little bit, I decided to hit with him. Stickball had given me great eye-to-ball coordination and I just imagined that the racquet was a stickball bat that was very wide at one end. After about ten minutes, I had learned to hit the ball well enough to give my partner a decent workout. I also discovered something else – I liked squash. I began to practice every day in between my locker duties and my break from homework.

After a few weeks, I was able to play reasonably well. The word got around that "the locker kid can play squash" and members began to call on a frequent basis to book games with me when their regular squash partners were not available. I became the de facto club pro. The club loved it. It gave them another member service at no additional cost.

During the winters of my college years, I would leave New York late on Thursday nights and either hitchhike or drive to Vermont where I worked from Friday to Monday as part of the ski patrol at Bromley Mountain. I loved this job. I would get up at 5:00 a.m. every day and ride the Snowcat up the mountain long before the lifts opened. I had learned to ski during high school. I didn't ski with tremendous style, but, given my background in sports, I was strong and rarely fell – good qualifications for any member of a ski patrol. I was driven to become a better skier, so I skied constantly. I was usually the first on the mountain and almost always the last off. I skied when it was ten below zero. I skied in the rain. By the time I graduated from college, I had become a good skier.

After college, I decided to take some time off before launching myself into a career, so I moved to Vermont and took a full-time job at Bromley Mountain. By now I skied well enough to race, and I eventually became a professional instructor.

One Easter Sunday morning, I was involved in making a ski film. While doing a Royal Christie (skiing on only one ski with the other raised behind me so that it rested on my shoulder), I fell. The ski didn't release, but my leg did. I broke the tibia. While the cast was being put on, I gave a lot of thought to my immediate future as a $180-per-week ski instructor with a hard-earned college degree and determined that it was time to move on.

The following Monday morning, I did one of the dumbest things I had done to date in my life. I sent a telegram (we didn't have e-mail then!) to the head of personnel at American Airlines at LaGuardia Airport. The telegram told him who I was, provided a minimal amount of personal background, and I stated that I was now "ready" for American Airlines to hire me. I was so naïve that I wasn't even aware of how presumptuous I was being. It just seemed like the thing to do at the time.

As it turned out, this guy had never received such an unusual request for employment. Out of sheer curiosity, he replied with a telegram asking me to come in at 9:00 a.m. the following week for an interview.

On Tuesday, I arrived at LaGuardia about an hour early. As luck would have it, I hobbled into the building from the parking lot with the man I was to meet. Of course, I did not recognize him, even as he held the door open for me, crutches and all. I asked him if he knew where I might find Personnel. He did.

Under the circumstances, the interview went very well. It turned out that the personnel manager was an avid skier who actually skied at Bromley and we knew many of the same people. We got on like old friends. He offered me an entry-level position as a management understudy. Management understudy was a trainee position where you could expect to be promoted to a supervisor in three years. I accepted and two weeks later started class to become a ticket agent at LaGuardia.

My immediate supervisor was a very tough customer. He didn't take lip from anybody. I will always remember his calling me into his office on the first day of training. It was a small office and had no decorations of any kind except for a framed slogan on the wall behind his desk. That slogan read: "If you hide your light under a bushel, you can't be seen from above." He gave me the once-over and glanced at my very slim personnel file. Then he asked why I thought I should be in his understudy group. I glanced at the slogan behind him and told him it was because I was far and away the best candidate for the job. He thought about that for a moment and then went on with the interview.

As he outlined the management understudy program, I realized that it would take me three years before I could hope to be promoted. Given my Type "A" personality, this was clearly far too long for me to wait. I had decided that the normal career path at American was not for me and I would have to do something different.

I was in training for the next two months and then became a ticket agent. The day I started as a ticket agent I also started my own promotion plan. This plan has served me well for my entire business career. In essence, the plan was simple, although in execution it required extra work on a daily basis. The plan was to immediately select the next job I wanted and establish a course of action to quickly get that job. Basically, I would learn as much about that job as the person currently holding the position and be sure that management knew it. When the job became available (and they always do), I had an edge since management knew that I was more qualified than any of the other candidates.

The results of this strategy quickly became evident. I was promoted in three months rather than three years. I will give you one example of how this worked for me: When I was manager for American Airlines at LaGuardia Airport, I wanted to move into sales in the New York region. I felt that having both an operations and a sales background would be best for my career, so I contacted a sales rep and offered to come in on one of my mid-week days off to make joint sales calls on his corporate travel managers. I usually worked weekends at the airport and took Mondays and Tuesdays off. The rep immediately responded to this as it gave him another great reason to visit his accounts. Having a contact at the airport was important to his corporate travel people since I could V.I.P. their officers, help them when flights were sold out, and smooth things over during bad weather.

For the next three months, I made joint calls on one of my days off with almost every sales rep in the New York region. Sure enough, an opening occurred in the region and the district sales manager asked his staff for replacement suggestions. The entire staff told him: "Capozzi knows the job, the customers, the paperwork, and the staff better than anyone." With almost 50 candidates applying for the position, I was offered the job.

The day I started this job I also started working on my next promotion which was to become the national sales manager at American's hotel division which was then called Americana Hotels. I used the exact same approach and was promoted in less than a year. I had a total of eight promotions in my eight years at American Airlines.

I left American as a senior director in the marketing department at their corporate headquarters to take a position as vice president of sales for a division of Midland Bank. I stayed at Midland for five years and was promoted five times until I became CEO of the North American division and a member of the board of directors managing a $400 million profit center.

Five years after I joined the Midland Bank Group, my son was born. We had 900 offices in 143 countries and I was traveling about 20 days each month all around the world. I did not want my son to grow up not knowing his father, so I decided to quit a great job. I didn't know what I was going to do but I had brought in almost $100 million in new business for my company, so I had the confidence I could earn a living going on my own.

I started my current investment banking business in the basement of our brownstone in New York City. Over the course of the next two years, I formed a variety of companies such as an exposition company that ran shows at the New York Coliseum; a construction company that renovated and sold brownstones in New York City; a consulting company that did work for the United Nations, the Ford Foundation and others; and a management recruitment company with a half dozen Fortune 500 clients.

Two years later, my wife had her second bout with cancer and Memorial Sloan-Kettering Hospital gave her six months to live. My daughter had just been born, my son was now two years old, and we were devastated. We decided to sell our home and all of our businesses and move with our children to a country home with lots of land in Connecticut to live a simpler life. After liquidating everything, we ended up with a few million dollars, and I retired. Somehow my wife survived her bout with cancer. To this day, none of her doctors understand it. However, I learned that quality of life and family were very important issues to me. I had become the world's best gardener, an expert at doing the laundry, knew all the checkers at the supermarkets by their first name, and was known as "Mr. Mom" by the kids at school. I had not worn a tie in three years. I bought a backhoe and a pick-up truck and didn't even own a car. My son actually learned to drive using the backhoe.

Three years after I had retired, a funny thing happened. I had just watched the *Today Show* and realized it was 10:00 a.m. and I was still in my pajamas. I also realized it was time for me to go back to work, so I started my investment banking business again. My primary activity was raising capital for start-up ventures. I took both a personal equity position in almost every business I funded and an active role in the marketing of most of them.

With respect to the business ventures in which I have become involved, I have always followed a simple plan: first, identify wants and needs in a particular market, then develop a marketing plan to fulfill those wants and needs, provide the capital to start a business to execute the solution, bring in the right people to manage the business, and then sell the business once it is established. If you can indeed get a business that works off the ground, you can always find a buyer. I have started and sold food companies, alarm and security companies, marketing companies, investment companies, and even a telecommunications company. I really don't think it matters what kind of business you start – the key is to identify specific customer wants and needs and find a profitable way to provide a solution. Once you have found it, you have accomplished the first (and most important) step in building a business. I call it a "sound business proposition." From it, everything else flows.

Another thing I have learned is that, when starting a business, it is best to form "virtual corporations" if you can. These are entities that require a minimal amount of operating capital and rely primarily on the expert resources of others. For example, a few years ago I started a food company. It was a "better for you" food products company that was launched before Nabisco started SnackWell's.

The "wants and needs" within the market were for snacks that were fat-free, but tasted good. Normally, with "better for you" foods the box tastes better than the product. I felt if I could find a way to make fat-free taste good, we could build a great business. My wife's background was food. She grew up in the restaurant business, was a French-trained chef, and held senior positions in American Airlines' food division.

I asked her to see if she could create fat-free snacks that tasted good, and she thought she could. I recruited a group of the foremost scientists in the field to work with her, and after months of work she created a line of great tasting, fat-free brownies and cookies. They also contained no additives, no preservatives, and could last six months on a retail shelf without getting stale or moldy – not an easy task.

I then invested $500,000 and formed the Greenfield Healthy Foods Company. I explored a variety of bakeries and contracted with Flowers Baking, one of the largest and finest companies in the baking industry, to produce our products. I hired a group of young executives who had experience in food, distribution, marketing, and finance to run our company. We used independent food distributors to bring our products to grocery stores. In a few years, we were in almost every major market in America.

Once the company got started, I raised another $2 million from outside investors to fund it until we achieved positive cash flow. We ended up with a business that had no buildings, no factories, no equipment, no trucks, no drivers ... and very little overhead. We even farmed out all of our accounts receivable and accounts payable. We had created the quintessential "virtual corporation."

Our business plan identified that if we were successful in our marketing efforts, we should try to sell our business in five years because it would take the competition about that long to figure out what we were doing and copy us. So, almost five years to the day, we sold our company to the Campbell Soup Company for millions of dollars ...

and sure enough, within a year of our sale, there were eight major food companies in the market (like Nabisco with SnackWell's) with fat-free brownies and cookies that tasted good. I can honestly say, however, that none ever tasted as good as ours.

By the time we totally exited Greenfield, our sales exceeded $52 million and we were in 67,000 grocery, convenience, and health food stores across America. Of importance, we never paid a penny in slotting fees. I have been asked by large colleges to create a case study about Greenfield, but I haven't done it yet. Perhaps, if I ever retire again, I might do it.

I hope you enjoy the maxims and anecdotes I have created and collected in this book. It is my hope that they spark something within you that allows you to move ahead and be successful in your business career as well as to enhance your personal life.

1

Suggest solutions when you present problems and you'll pave the way to your own promotion.

2

Your competence level is directly related to your confidence level.

3

In all my years in business, I have found that people in meetings tend to agree on decisions that, as individuals, they know are dumb.

4

Never assume that the customer can't afford what you are offering.

5

Smart executives know that they do the things they need to do when they need to do them, so someday they can do the things they want to do when they want to do them.

6

Corporate life is not always fair,
but you should be.

7

Always start out by asking for
more than you really need.

8

The ability to recognize ability is a very rare ability.

9

YOU ARE KNOWN BY THE FRIENDS YOU KEEP AND THE DECISIONS YOU MAKE

Several years ago, I submitted a membership application for a very close Jewish friend at my very prestigious club located in Manhattan. Subsequently, I was contacted by a member of the Admissions Committee who asked me to withdraw my application because "we don't want Jewish members." I couldn't believe my ears, immediately handed him my membership card, and have never been back since. In my business career, I have found that I always do better when I don't compromise my values. To this day my friend is still my friend and, guess what? I found another club to join that didn't make me feel uncomfortable.

10
IF YOU HAVEN'T LEARNED HOW
NOT TO DO THINGS, DON'T LEARN

Peter Rogers is an investor in several of my companies and sits on a variety of my boards. He has been the president or chairman of many very successful companies, including Nabisco. He's also one of the brightest marketing people I have ever met and while he doesn't have an M.B.A., he does have a B.S. and a Ph.D. He sent me the following story which I would like to share with you:

In the mid-1980s, when I was appointed president of Nabisco Brands USA – a $6 billion group of businesses comprised of companies such as Del Monte, The Nabisco Biscuit Company, Nabisco Foods, Planters Peanut Company, Lifesavers, and others – I was asked a very simple question, "How on earth did you get to be where you are without having an M.B.A.?"

My response was: "Because I was never taught how *not* to do things. I practice the art of the possible." What I meant by this was really a modest condemnation of the typical M.B.A. curriculum of the 1960s through the early 1980s. In those days, most M.B.A. candidates were taught by the case study method, a technique based on analysis, most of which was numerical. This method of teaching, coupled with early life experiences in multiple-choice examination methods, leads students to study those aspects of a business that can be quantified and are amenable to numerical analysis. Non-tangible aspects such as timing, judgment, leadership, and just "plain luck" are often not subject to critical scrutiny, and yet these are often the most critical "keys to success" in a business. Practicing the art of the possible, putting reasonable reliance on intuition, judgment, and "accumulated wisdom" is often a necessary counter-balance to pure analytical analysis of the quantifiable aspects of a business situation. Thus, it is not always necessary to have an M.B.A. in order to be able to lead, excite, motivate, and discipline.

11
All executives make fewer mistakes
when their mouths are shut.

12
"Nearly every man who develops an idea works it up to the point where it looks impossible, and then gets discouraged. That is not the place to become discouraged."
– Thomas Edison

The executive who works from 8 a.m.
to 8 p.m. every day will be both very
wealthy and fondly remembered by his
widow's next husband.

14

Better is always better than bigger.

15

One difference in working for yourself is the level of your goals. When you work for yourself, you set high goals and try to exceed them. When you work for someone else you set lower goals and try to achieve them.

16

You know you're working too hard when the night cleaning lady invites you to her daughter's wedding.

17

THERE IS ALWAYS A RIGHT WAY AND A WRONG WAY TO SUCCEED

Two Jesuit priests both wanted a cigarette while they prayed. They decided to ask their bishop for permission. The first asked but was told, "No." A little while later he spotted his friend smoking. "Why did the Bishop allow you to smoke and not me?" he asked. The friend replied, "Because you asked if you could smoke while you prayed and I asked if I could pray while I smoked."

18

Keep a pad and pencil by your bed. Some of your most creative ideas come at night.

19

Success is getting what you want;
happiness is wanting what you get.

20

Wealth comes to those who make things happen;
not to those who let things happen.

21

No executive can value the worth of others
unless he first learns to value himself.

22

Age is a function of mind over matter ...
and if you don't mind, it doesn't matter.

23

A good salesperson can sell a bridge
where there is no water.

24

Attitude is a little thing that makes a big difference.

25

Only a fool tries to build his reputation
on the things he plans to do.

26

Speak when you're angry and you'll make the best
speech you'll ever regret.

27

Problems that appear to be easy to solve always
belong to someone else.

28

Never slow dance with your boss' spouse
at the annual Christmas party.

29

Any businessman who has ever failed at something
should remember that even in baseball you can
strike-out two out of three times at bat and still
make a million dollars a year.

30

God gave us two ends: one to sit on and the other to think with. Success depends on which end we use the most.

31

In a speech, make each point three times.

32

If you want it tomorrow, ask for it yesterday.

33

IN BUSINESS, DON'T WORRY ABOUT HOW YOU LOOK – WORRY ABOUT HOW YOU ACT

Historically, world leaders who are remembered for their accomplishments are rarely remembered for their appearance ... or lack thereof. Most have been rather common looking. Consider Abraham Lincoln. He attended a party one night and overheard a rather stuffy woman comment on his appearance: "He is a very common-looking man." Lincoln responded: "The Lord prefers common-looking people. That is the reason he makes so many of them."

ANALYZE THE FACTS
BEFORE MAKING KEY DECISIONS
On June 25, 1876, General George
Armstrong Custer received information
that a significant number of Indians were
gathering at Little Big Horn. Without
analyzing the facts, he decided to ride out
with 250 men to "surround" almost 3,000
Indians. This was a serious mistake!

35

Executives who want their employees to have their feet on the ground must first put some responsibility on their shoulders.

36

If you smell horse crap when you enter the barn, look around and you'll probably find a horse's ass. If the same seems true in your meetings, it might be time to fix the problem.

37

THOSE WHO SUCCEED IN BUSINESS KNOW THEIR LIMITS AND KNOW HOW TO GO BEYOND THOSE LIMITS

A while ago, the famous photographer Annie Leibowitz published a wonderful study of Olympic portraits. In an interview on the *Today Show* she described sprinter Dennis Mitchell as "so fast that when I developed my film he wasn't there!" Annie then moved her lens further forward so that Mitchell and the shutter arrived in the same place at the same time and she captured an absolutely amazing shot of the world class sprinter.

38
Do Your Work At Work

Many businesspeople have unsuccessful marriages or poor relationships with their children because they have never learned to do their work at work.

In business, if we want to win, we plan carefully, execute properly, and follow up on a very timely basis. To have a successful relationship with your spouse or children, you must also plan, execute, and follow up with the same degree of effort as you do in your corporate life.

What would your boss think about you if you missed every important function? Why should your kids hold you in high regard if you miss all of their games or school functions? Do you think you would get the next promotion if you were to arrive late for every company meeting? Why should your spouse feel great about you if you are never home on time?

John Cleese is credited with the story of a man doing paperwork in bed late into the evening. Trying to sleep, his very aggravated wife finally challenged him to turn off the light and go to sleep. He explained that he couldn't because he had to finish his work. She asked the key question: "Why don't you do your work at work?" His reply: "I can't, I am at meetings all day."

Now, really curious, she questioned: "Well, when do you sleep?" His reply: "I sleep in meetings like everyone else!"

Try to avoid distractions or unproductive meetings that consume your time if you really want to succeed. The truly successful businessperson learns how to get his or her work done at work.

39
A free lunch is only found in mousetraps.

40
"It's the law of the universe that the strong shall survive and the weak must fall by the way, and I don't care what idealistic plan is cooked up, nothing can change that."
– Walt Disney

41
Fortunately, an employee's mind once stretched by creative thinking, never regains its original size.

42

To succeed, be daring, be first, be different.

43

The smart executive is the one who knows what he should do ... the smarter executive is the one who knows what he shouldn't do.

44

An executive's greatest reward for success is not what he's paid for it, but what he becomes because of it.

45
DON'T BLAME THE TOMATOES

If a gardener plants tomatoes and they don't grow, the smart gardener doesn't blame the tomatoes but immediately investigates the source of the problem: not enough sun, needs more water, may need fertilizer.

When a business isn't growing, the smart executive shouldn't fire his employees but investigate the source of the problem: competition, pricing, quality, distribution, etc. Once management knows what's wrong, solutions can be attempted.

Ben Frankly says ...

"If all your company executives always agree with everything the boss says, you could probably fire half of them and never notice the difference."

47

Eighty percent of success is showing up.

48

The best way to appreciate your job
is to be without it for awhile.

49

"Genius is one percent inspiration
and ninety-nine percent perspiration."
– Thomas Edison

50

**IN BUSINESS, AS IN LIFE, IF YOU FALL DOWN
GET UP AND KEEP GOING IF YOU WANT TO WIN**
Bonny St. John Dean was born with one leg – that
never stopped her. She excelled at everything she
did, including getting a job in the White House.
She even learned to ski with one leg. She became
so good that she participated in the 1984 Para-
Olympics in Innsbrook, Austria. During the race
she fell, but immediately got up and kept going.
She took third and won a Bronze Medal. When told
that the Gold Medal winner also fell on the course,
she commented that, "if you fall down, you can still
win the Gold ... just be sure to get up faster!"

51

An idea can turn to dust or magic,
depending on the talent with which you rub it.

52

VERY FEW OF US NEVER MAKE MISTAKES
During a fiery exchange at a summit meeting
between President Kennedy and Premier Kruschev,
Kennedy asked the Russian Premier: "Do you ever
admit to a mistake?"

"Certainly I do," Kruschev responded. "In a speech
before the 20th Party Congress I admitted all of
Stalin's mistakes."

To be successful in business you must recognize
your mistakes – if only not to make them again.

53

"You may have achieved price and selection parity,
but the experts say, and our customers confirm,
Customer Service is the next battleground in
retailing."
> – Dale C. Pond
> Senior Executive Vice President,
> Marketing/Merchandising
> Lowe's

54

Products need people to survive.

55

When the going gets easy, it's time for a reality check ... you might be going downhill.

56

A Sign Of The Times

As a boy I started my first job at age 10, selling soda at a construction site. At 14 I set pins at a manual bowling alley, sold hot dogs at 15, and worked in construction at 16. I couldn't wait for "snow days" – not because I didn't have to go to school, but because I could shovel snow from 6:00 a.m. to 8:00 p.m. and make what was then a fortune.

When my son was 16 years old, I had him working every summer in an effort to instill in him a strong work ethic. One day I asked him to help me build a shed behind my barn. I told him that someday he would have his own place and he would need to know how to build things. His response was: "I'm not going to do that. I am going to earn a lot of money and hire someone to do that!"

57

Always try to pick up the "cheap" lunch tabs.

58

We do not stop working because we are old;
we grow old because we stop working.

59

In business, people take different roads to achieve success. Just because they're not on your road doesn't mean they've gotten lost.

60

SUCCESSFUL LEADERSHIP DEPENDS ON ONE'S ABILITY TO MAKE PEOPLE WANT TO FOLLOW RATHER THAN HAVE TO FOLLOW

General Eisenhower used to demonstrate the art of leadership with a simple piece of string. He'd put it on a table and say: "Pull it and it'll follow wherever you wish. Push it and it will go nowhere." Managers who prod rather than lead rarely obtain the maximum performance from their employees.

In business, as in life, if you stand in the middle of the road your chances of being run over are doubled.

62
Never go to a meeting unprepared.

63
You'll learn more about a road by traveling it than by consulting all the maps in the world.

64
The first step you should take if you want to be successful is to decide what kind of executive you are. Executives fall into three categories: Those who make things happen; those who watch things happen; and those who wonder what happened.

65
Find a job you really enjoy
and you'll add five days to every week of your life.

66
The difference between an employee that says "Let me do that for you" and one that says "That's not my job" is that the latter should be working for your biggest competitor.

67
"Long-Term Success Is A Result Of
A Series Of Short-Term Successes."

As I write this book I can't help thinking about many of the people that have contributed to its content. It will be interesting to look back in ten or twenty years to see how many have moved up the corporate ladder. The above maxim was sent to me by Steven S. Reinemund, who was then the chairman and CEO, Frito-Lay Company, and I included it in my first book. Years ago, Steve had stayed overnight in our home and I can remember discussing business, kids, and life in general in my kitchen over Belgian Waffles. What struck me most was his tremendous value system and integrity – even more than his professionalism in business. I mentioned seven years ago that:

> Steve is someone that will continue to move up the corporate ladder and in his case I really believe "up" is totally indefinable. If you invest in any company that is run by Steve Reinemund, you will not lose. His above maxim about long term success is so correct and so very "Reinemund."

I find it interesting that in about seven years, Steve did "move up the corporate ladder" – he became chairman of PepsiCo.

68

People who wait for all conditions to be perfect before acting, never act.

69

"Follow up is the Chariot of Genius."
– Terry Lierman
Former President
Capital Associates, Inc.
Washington, D.C.

70

Most stockholders recognize that it's better to live within your means ... even if you have to borrow money to do it.

71

Sometimes the things we get for nothing
end up costing us the most.

72

Financing ... get as much as you can the first time out. It's much more expensive the next time.

73

Almost no quality products sell for a cheap price.

74

Don't be in a hurry to become successful;
you might just rush right past it.

75

ANSWER THE NEED, NOT JUST THE QUESTION

My friend Jack Kliger, who is now the president of Hachette and manages one of the largest publishing entities in the world, still finds the time to be involved in substantial community service work – a great role model for all of us. He shared the following with me:

> When I was being trained as a sales rep, an old pro took me out to "show me the ropes." He first stopped into a candy store and asked the proprietor for a flint for his cigarette lighter. The owner said he didn't carry them; we turned around and left. As soon as we got out, the old pro looked at me and asked: "What did he do wrong?" I said I didn't know. The pro said: "He didn't try to sell me matches!"

Ben Frankly says ...

"You never get a second chance
to make a good first impression."

77

The best time to save some money
is when you have some.

78

Be careful.
Sometimes when you poke a snake, it will bite you.

79

"Most folks are about as happy
as they make up their minds to be."
– Abraham Lincoln

80

"Everything should be made as simple as possible,
but not simpler."
– Albert Einstein

81

"I haven't failed … I've just found 10,000 ways that
don't work."
– Benjamin Franklin

82

Consider customer complaints as opportunities. At least you can try to salvage these customers ... but what about the ones who don't complain and just go away?

83

Not deciding is deciding to do nothing.

84

If you are making a commission, say so upfront.

85

HIRE EMPLOYEES WITH DIFFERENT STRENGTHS

I've started a lot of businesses and have learned that we all have a natural tendency to surround ourselves with employees who think and act the same way we do. We instinctively want everyone to be our friends. This isn't always the best policy for building a business. Try to hire the most effective staff. Build a complementary team in which your employees' strengths balance out your weaknesses.

86

"Good people don't exist well
in a bad environment."
– Sue Galati

87

All criticism should be constructive.

88

It isn't the employees you terminate who make your
life miserable; it's the ones you don't.

89

"The test of our progress is not whether we add
more to the abundance of those who have much; it
is whether we provide enough for those who have
too little."
– Franklin D. Roosevelt

90

We are continually faced with great opportunities
brilliantly disguised as insoluble problems.

91

Remember, creditors have much better memories than debtors.

92

The best way to convince a foolish executive he is wrong is to let him have his way.

93
SUCCESS REQUIRES FOCUS

Charlie McCarthy, former chief operating officer, Tetley USA, Inc., is about the best operations executive I have ever met and he has a wonderful way with people. Because he has been president of Campbell Soup Company and president of Pepperidge Farm, I have a great deal of respect for Charlie's advice. Over dinner one night he told me the following:

> In business, our challenge is to put all of our activities into one of three buckets. The first contains those things that add value to our lives and our companies. The second contains activities that keep our business steady and orderly. And third is for all those other things that everybody asks you to do. Successful leaders spend most of their time working on bucket number one. I also call it "focus!"

"Mind if I play through?"

95
TRY TO EARN WHAT THE JOB IS WORTH

Recently I had lunch with a close friend who was leaving a senior position at a major Fortune 500 Company. He had been with this company for 17 years and had never gone through "the job search" process. Over the course of two hours we talked about every aspect of finding a new job. At one point I told him that my philosophy about compensation is to be paid what the job is worth. I strongly believe companies could reduce significant employee turnover if they simply paid their people a fair and correct compensation. I also believe if someone is rude enough to ask you your current salary, you have the right to be rude enough to tell them the number you "think" the job is really worth. What you are earning at your current position is totally your business and the management at a new prospective company really has no right to even ask about your current financial affairs. The interviewer should know what his or her job is worth and should tell you the amount they are willing to pay you based upon the scope and responsibilities of their job and your résumé experience.

I counseled my friend to mention a salary that he thought the new position was worth if the situation arose, knowing his current company would never give out confidential compensation information to any outsiders for verification.

About two weeks later, I received a huge basket of fruit from my friend. I called him thinking it was a "thanks for taking two hours of my time" gift, but he told me it was for my specific advice. As it turned out, he did well on a job interview with the president of a new company and was offered a position. The president then asked him what his "current" salary was. Remembering our lunch conversation, my friend gave him a number he believed his new job was really worth, which was about $100,000 more than he was currently making. The president thought for a moment and said: "Okay, the position is well within that range, and I can also give you an additional 30% as an incentive to join us."

96

Spread authority over many people and decisions will be made much more efficiently.

97

The customer who has been pleased by a company tells an average of three people about it. The customer who has had a problem with a company tells an average of ten people about it.

98

Better to ask twice than to lose your way once.

99

What Goes Around Comes Around

In 1872 George Westinghouse, the famous inventor, received his first patent for an automatic air brake that worked far better than the brakes currently being used on trains. He wrote to Cornelius Vanderbilt, president of the New York Central Railroad, identifying the advantages of his new invention. Vanderbilt returned his letter but wrote across the bottom: "I have no time to waste on fools."

Westinghouse then approached the Pennsylvania Railroad who immediately became interested in his invention and funded further development. News of the success of the air brake reached Vanderbilt who wrote Westinghouse a letter asking him to set up a meeting. Westinghouse sent the letter back to Vanderbilt with the notation, "I have no time to waste on fools," scrawled across the bottom.

Vanderbilt eventually purchased air brakes from Westinghouse at a greatly increased price.

100

You can't be seen if you stay in your office.

101

One of God's greatest miracles is to enable ordinary people to do extraordinary things.

102

Try not to argue with someone when he is right.

103

The smart executive never allows his employees to complain about a problem unless they offer a solution.

104

IMAGE IS IMPORTANT

At a New York party, Muhammad Ali, the world heavyweight boxing champion, was introduced to violinist Isaac Stern. Stern remarked: "You might say we're in the same business ... we both earn a living with our hands." Ali replied: "You must be pretty good; there isn't a mark on you."

Ben Frankly says ...

"Any problem you can solve with a check
isn't a problem ... it's an expense."

106
Ability is nothing without opportunity.

107
In business, as in forest fires,
big problems always start out small.

108
Successful executives learn to forgive and forget their
enemies ... they also keep a record of their names.

109
"Always swing hard,
in case you happen to hit the ball."
– Duke Snider

110
REALLY, WHAT IS FAILURE?
Most inventors tell you that they try about 999
times to make an invention work. Once it does,
they do very well. The successful inventor treats
his failures simply as practice shots.

111

Don't piss off a crocodile,
until after you've crossed the river.

112

AT THE CORE OF EVERY BIG PROBLEM IS A SIMPLE SOLUTION

A number of years ago, when I was just starting out in business, I was fortunate to have a friend who taught me how to reduce very complex situations to simple ones. His lesson involved stepping back and not getting caught up in tons of detail. One such lesson involved analyzing a business that was losing money. This business had seven operating divisions. My mentor asked his chief financial officer to spread out the P&Ls for each division on the boardroom table. The first thing he did was to pick up the four P&Ls that were in the black. He then told the CFO that if we simply removed the three divisions that were losing money, all we would have left were those divisions that were making a profit – problem solved. After all was said and done, he did get rid of two of the divisions and brought the third into the black.

113

Always make the most of the best
and the least of the worst.

114

FOLLOW THE SIMPLE FORK
IN THE ROAD TO SUCCESS

Thomas Edison was very skilled in hiring executives, particularly when hiring engineers. In one unique test, he would give an applicant an empty cup and ask: "How much water will it hold?"

Obviously, there were two ways to find the answer. One way was to utilize your skills as an engineer and via the use of special gauges, measure the surface area of the cup and then convert this data to identify volume. This could take almost 30 minutes to accomplish.

The other method was to simply fill the cup with water and pour the contents into a standard measuring cup. Time to accomplish this feat? About 30 seconds.

Engineers who utilized their skills via the first route were thanked politely and dismissed. Those who chose the simple route were hired.

THE HEIGHT OF YOUR ALTITUDE
WILL BE DETERMINED BY YOUR ATTITUDE,
NOT YOUR APTITUDE

A number of years ago, I had the pleasure of doing business with Gary L. Harrison who ran the specialty baking group for Flowers Industries, a multibillion dollar food company that owned Keebler, Mrs. Smith's, and many others.

Gary and I became good friends and I have always admired his attitude and judgment in business. One story in particular that comes to mind is his philosophy about co-packing. He would produce products for anyone – even his biggest competitors. He felt that it was more important to get the maximum utilization possible out of his plant, people, and equipment, than it was to worry about his competitors being in the market with him. I will always remember his comment:

"Hell, if I don't make products for them, they'll just go someplace else, and if I can't stop them from competing with me I might as well make something on the production side."

Gary will always be successful in business because he has a winning attitude, and a clarity of direction that all highly successful executives require. He sent me the above maxim and I know it is one reason he is so successful.

"You're definitely hitting it farther with
that new driver, Sam."

117

An executive who swears he has never made a mistake works for a boss who has made a big one.

118

In business it's nice to be important,
but to be respected, it's important to be nice.

119

Don't ever think about how good you are;
think about how great you can be.

120
TRY NOT TO ARGUE
WITH SOMEONE SMARTER THAN YOU

As a young man, Winston Churchill sported a mustache. At a political dinner he got into an argument with an older woman who, attempting to put him down, commented: "Mr. Churchill, I care for neither your politics nor your mustache." "Madam," responded Churchhill, "you are quite unlikely to come into contact with either."

121
THERE'S NO SUCH THING AS A STUPID IDEA

Along the way in my business career, I have met some wonderful and stimulating people that I have really enjoyed working with. One such person is Ted Giannitti, Jr., who was the chief financial officer at Greenfield, a company I started and ultimately sold to the Campbell Soup Company. Ted gave me his thoughts on brainstorming which I hope you agree with:

> I worked for someone earlier in my career that practiced the concept: "There's no such thing as a stupid idea." In meetings, our entire staff would be encouraged to suggest anything that came to mind that would improve our business. The first time someone laughed at a suggestion, the boss asked him to leave the meeting. From that point on, we all knew it was okay to suggest anything without intimidation. I witnessed some of the stupidest ideas begin to develop into magnificent "out of the box" concepts. People got excited and statements like "great, but what if we added this or did that ..." followed. Positive feedback generates new ideas, stimulates creative expression, and allows every employee to actually participate in all levels of business.

122

Nothing is interesting if you're not interested.

123

The greatest tragedy in business is not that you tried and failed, but that you failed to try.

124

Exercise your body – it will build up your mind.

125

Winning executives see an answer for every problem. Losing executives see a problem for every answer.

126

"If a man is called to be a street sweeper, he should sweep streets even as Michelangelo painted, or Beethoven composed music, or Shakespeare wrote poetry. He should sweep streets so well that all the hosts of heaven and earth will pause to say: 'Here lived a great street sweeper who did his job well.'"
– Martin Luther King, Jr.

127

When considering a new supervisor for your shipping department, give him an open road map and see if he can fold it up again. If he can, hire him.

128

The issue is not the anger; it's how you express it.

129

Remember, you spend at least eight hours of your day with your secretary and only about three hours a day with your wife ... and your wife knows it. Send a gift once in a while for no reason at all ... to your wife.

130
MUSHROOM MANAGEMENT

If you leave your employees in the dark, constantly give them lots of horse crap, and let them hibernate unattended for awhile, you'll have employees who are more like mushrooms than productive workers ... and the best thing they can then hope for is to be canned.

"I want to show you the new vacuum
that your neighbor just told me you
couldn't afford."

132
Call everyone back.

133
Don't brag; it's not the whistle that moves the train.

134
"The journey of a thousand miles
starts with a single step."
– Chinese Proverb

135
"Well done is always better than well said."
– Benjamin Franklin

136
HE WHO LAUGHS FIRST
DOESN'T ALWAYS LAUGH LAST
George Bernard Shaw, the famous playwright, sent Winston Churchill two tickets to the opening of his play, *Saint Joan*, with a note: "Am reserving two tickets for you for my première. Come and bring a friend – if you have one." Churchill replied that he regretted being unable to attend the opening, but asked if it would be possible to have tickets for the second night – "If there is one."

137
IF YOU'RE GIVEN THE PROBLEM, SOLVE IT

In my book, *A Spirit of Greatness; Stories from the Employees of American Airlines*, Sales Manager Carl Wimmer related a story of his co-worker who took a personal interest in resolving a company problem:

Kathy Bagley worked for American Airlines in sales. At one point she was asked to make special arrangements for a severely disabled boy in a custom-designed wheelchair who was traveling with his family. Kathy made all of the necessary special handling arrangements with the airports and the trip was a success. However, upon the return it was discovered that the wheelchair was damaged beyond repair. Kathy researched what was needed to get a replacement wheelchair and worked with American and the manufacturer to ensure that the boy had a new chair a day or two later.

Kathy is the type of employee who sees beyond the scope of the job description – an employee who can manage a situation quickly and efficiently and has the persistence to see it through to its resolution. Any employee who uses their brain as well as the job manual to resolve a problem is welcome on my team.

138
Ask questions.

139
No one ever drowned in their own sweat.

140
One difference between most successful executives and most unsuccessful ones is that with unsuccessful executives, when all is said and done, more is said than done.

141
Job security is being worth
more than you're getting paid.

142
"There are two types of employees: Those who do the work and those who take the credit. Try to be in the first group; there is much less competition there."
– Indira Gandhi

143

When weighing the faults of others,
be careful not to put your thumb on the scale.

144

When interviewing a new candidate, ask yourself
how you'd feel if the person were working for your
largest competitor rather than you.

145

"It's not just whether it's legal or illegal;
it's whether it's right or wrong."
– Ralph Giannola
Former Vice President, Marketing
Marriott Corporation

146

The very smart executive is smarter than most other
people, and smart enough not to tell them so.

147

It is easier to accept difficult people if you
recognize that most of them feel so small inside that
they need to act big and obnoxious outside.

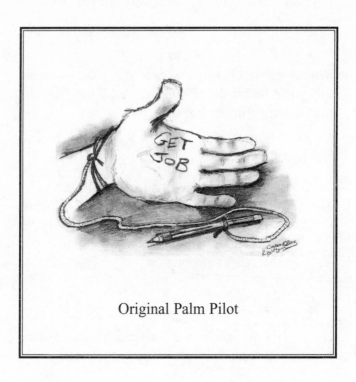

Original Palm Pilot

149

Enemies can indeed come back to haunt you.
Sometimes it just takes a little time.

150

If you are not sure that you'll need it long term, rent it.

151

"Nobody ever got into trouble
by keepin' his mouth shut."
– Forrest Gump

152

To grow your business, don't tell employees how to
do the job, tell them what needs to be done.

153

"It takes years to build a reputation for integrity but
it only takes a poor decision and a brief moment to
lose it forever."
– Richard R. Fogarty
Former Chairman and CEO
Labatt USA

154

Don't wear your best suit to a union negotiation.

155

"I know it's wrong, but every once in a while, if you really get mad, it's okay to just stomp that sucker flat."
– Lyndon Baines Johnson

156

If there are things about a job candidate you don't like during the interview, you will like them even less after you hire him.

157

Respect people for who they are,
not what you want them to be.

158

"See nothing less than perfection because, even though that in itself might be an impossible goal, you will discover great things during the pursuit."
– Steven Wardell

159

Learn from the mistakes of others. You won't live long enough to make them all yourself.

160

If you play golf with your boss and win, he'll want to play again. If he doesn't, he'll probably fire you and it doesn't matter.

161

It always takes more effort to figure out what's right than what's wrong ... but the extra effort is always worth it.

162

Sometimes when you're holding a 900 lb. gorilla by the ankle, it's best to let him run away.

163

If you think education is expensive, wait 'til you see what ignorance costs you.

164
"… the devil hath power to assume a pleasing shape."
– William Shakespeare

165
If the hardest part of the job is finding a parking place, your employees may start parking in your biggest competitor's lot.

166
Avoid shortcuts.
They always take too much time in the long run.

167
SOMETIMES IT'S BEST
TO JUST MIND YOUR OWN BUSINESS
At a political dinner party a slightly intoxicated Winston Churchill became engaged in a heated exchange with a female member of Parliament. At the end of the exchange the lady scornfully remarked, "Mr. Churchill, you are drunk." Churchill replied: "And you, Madame, are ugly … but tomorrow I shall be sober."

The famous NFL coach Vince Lombardi
once said, "Practice does not make perfect.
Only perfect practice makes perfect."

169
DIG WHERE THE GOLD IS ...
UNLESS YOU JUST NEED SOME EXERCISE

Not long ago I was having dinner with the president of a large ad agency and I mentioned that one of the websites for *The New Yorker* Magazine contained a statement that "98% of *New Yorker* subscribers say they read the cartoons before anything else."

I thought about this and decided to do some research. Not only did we find that almost everyone indeed reads cartoons, but we validated that if we utilize the cartoon as an *advertising* element, rather than as a traditional editorial element, the readership impact and therefore the value, of the adjacent page significantly improves. If we put a client's brand directly on the cartoon the ROI for the advertiser is even greater.

We took our hypothesis to *Forbes* Magazine and following their review and similar conclusion created a new company called Jester Solutions. We signed a contract to create the "*Forbes* Moment of Humor" using humor to generate greater ROI for advertisers in a variety of ways.

We then approached *Golf Digest* and they came to the same conclusion. They also signed a contract with Jester Solutions to utilize humor to give advertisers more value for their dollars.

Taking the concept further, we tested humor in digital CRM programs and found that marketing or communication e-mail campaigns had as much as a 22% higher opening rate if the subject line contained the word "cartoon." What was really amazing was that almost 100% of the people in our test forwarded the e-mail cartoon to a friend or colleague. People forward jokes on the internet and if the cartoon is branded with a company name, the viral impact is beyond comprehension ... the forwarding or pass-along with exponential growth could go worldwide.

Lastly, we are now creating cartoons that contain brand integration in both the illustration and in the copy line.

Jester Solutions has recruited illustrators from across America and now has over 1,000 cartoons in its cartoon bank.

Jester is an example of how a business can be built from a simple opportunity – companies want greater efficiency, greater impact, and greater value for their advertising dollars. Jester simply gave them that.

You can read more about Jester on our website: www.jmcmarketingservices.com

170

Sometimes money just costs too much.

171

Frequent praise is always more effective than
frequent criticism.

172

If you have to downsize, first get rid of those
executives that think but never do and then get rid
of those that do but never think.

173

Try not to work for a company that makes or sells
anything you wouldn't want to give to your family
... life is just too short.

174

Great executives change their jobs for the sake of
their principles ... stupid ones change their
principles for the sake of their job.

175

Always pick up the lunch tab when you go out with your subordinates.

176

A Chain Is Only As Strong As Its Weakest Link

I realize that this is one of the oldest maxims in the known universe. But in the environment of business and corporate life that depends so much on teamwork, it bears repeating.

When I ran training seminars for new employees at American Airlines, I kept on returning to this old saw. I'd explain to the agents in my group that every day thousands of employees worked incredibly hard to ensure a passenger's loyalty to American Airlines. But if a reservation was wrong, or the ticket was written incorrectly, or the flight got out late, or the crew wasn't friendly, or the bag was missing, it didn't matter to the passenger that everything else was perfect. One mistake by one employee could mean that the work of thousands – from the corporate office to the maintenance hangars to the cockpit crew – had gone for naught.

Ben Frankly says ...

"Your desk should be a distribution center,
not a warehouse."

178

Experienced executives know that the quality of a hotel is directly proportionate to the thickness of the towels.

179

Perseverance is knocking long enough at the gate to wake someone up.

180

MOTIVATE YOUR EMPLOYEES
TO MOTIVATE YOUR BUSINESS

In almost every business I've started I've given my employees free equity. The difference in attitude and performance is amazing. When times were difficult, the average employee would have quit to find another job. The equity employee hung in there and made it work. I can honestly say that I have made almost a dozen employees millionaires during my business career, which makes me very happy. Even if you work for a company that won't allow you to give your team equity, it's still important to motivate them. Something as simple as giving them an upgraded title or a corner office with a window will make a huge difference ... to the employee and to your business.

181

In a meeting, never argue with a fool. Your boss may not know which one is which.

182

Only buy equipment at wholesale
that never needs to be fixed.

183

Ability is one of the most important strengths that any executive needs for success ... specifically, the ability to recognize ability in others.

184

The optimist finds opportunity in every difficulty; not difficulty in every opportunity.

185

Nothing kills employee morale and productivity faster than a boss who makes every decision. Give your staff the power and authority to grow and so will your business.

186
LITTLE THINGS DO MEAN A LOT

There is a story in my book, *A Spirit of Greatness; Stories from the Employees of American Airlines,* that illustrates the kind of personal employee commitment to a job (far beyond its requirements) that ultimately sets companies apart:

Ron Holthouser was a facilities maintenance mechanic for American Airlines. Ron speaks with such affection for his co-workers and his employment at American that I can't help but think that his positive attitude contributed greatly to his enjoyment of his job.

During his years with the company, Ron became aware that, through normal wear and tear, a significant number of baggage tags were becoming disconnected from luggage and lying on the floor under the baggage belt line. Ron was concerned about passengers' perception of American at the loss of their baggage tags, so he took it upon himself to do an extraordinary thing: Ron took the tags home, wrote a personal note of apology, and mailed the tags back to the passengers.

I can only imagine how surprised the customers were upon receiving their baggage tags and Ron's note. In fact, many began to return the favor and wrote notes of commendation back to Ron and to AA headquarters.

American Airlines rewarded Ron's outstanding commitment with a "Customer Comes First" award and watch.

Ron's personal investment in his company not only earned him praise within the organization, but certainly resulted in satisfied AA customers. In fact, a General Motors executive commented that following a prior bad experience with American, and upon receiving Ron's letter, he had changed his mind and had become an AA customer again.

Those in the head office may "steer" the company, but it is the everyday actions of each and every employee, at every level, that truly determine the success of a company.

187
"I count him braver who overcomes his desires than him who conquers his enemies; for the hardest victory is the victory over self."
– Aristotle

Spend the extra dollars to maintain your equipment. Remember, you don't have to brush all your teeth either … only the ones you want to keep!

189

A good scare is usually worth more
than good advice.

190

No matter what the circumstances, dress for success.

191

The next time you feel disappointed because you didn't get what you wanted, think about all the things you did get that you didn't want.

192

At a recent dinner with a friend who runs a Fortune 500 Company, he told me a story about a man who was voted "least likely to succeed" in high school but went on to become a multi-millionaire. When asked how he did it, he replied: "I produce my products for $1.25 each and sell them for $12.50 each … with my 10% mark-up I can't help but make lots of money."

Editor's Note: For those of you that majored in Liberal Arts rather than Finance, please read this twice.

193

No matter what the issue, no one ever won an argument with a customer.

194

In business it isn't hard to be smart from time to time. It's hard being smart all the time.

195

Some senior executives are really not more mature. They just have more money ... which makes them appear more mature.

196

When an executive retires and time is no longer as important, why does his company usually give him a gold watch?

197

The successful businessman will promise only what he can deliver ... then deliver more than he promised.

198

If someone is rushing you in an unreasonable fashion, tell them: "You can have it right, or you can have it now. You just can't have it right now."

199

Most happy executives are nice executives. If your boss is not such a nice boss, chances are he isn't very happy either.

200

Even if you are highly qualified, you must act the part in order to get the part. If you don't act like you can do the job, you probably won't get the job.

201

It doesn't matter if your name is on the outside of an office door or on your shirt pocket – everyone is important to the success of a company. The main difference, however, is that the guy with his name on the office door usually costs the company a lot more if he screws up.

202

Plotting revenge only allows the people
who hurt you to hurt you longer.

203

Sometimes the only way around the mountain
is to climb over it.

204

Business can actually be more dangerous than war.
In war, you can only be killed once, but in business
it can happen many times.

205

TEAMWORK IS A POWERFUL FORCE

A few years ago, I was riding in a chairlift with my
son while skiing in the French Alps. Suddenly,
about 100 yards away, an avalanche broke free from
the top of the mountain and roared down the slope.
It was a frightening experience. Upon reflection,
I thought about how delicate and fragile a single
snowflake is, and yet how powerful the force can
become when many snowflakes stick together.

Beware of the most dangerous person in business – the articulate incompetent.

QUICK THINKING SAVES THE DAY

Many years ago, I was employed by American Airlines in the New York sales office. I was successful in selling a charter to Mr. Harold Geneen, who was then chairman of ITT, for an executive meeting in London. As unbelievable as it might sound, we had 28 of the most senior ITT executives all on one plane and all at the same time. The charter was the first American Airlines flight to London and was sold as an ultra first class service. It contained the finest wines, thousands of dollars in gourmet meals, five movies, and the best cigars.

Our chief pilot flew left seat, our executive chef from the general office worked the galley and we had a doctor and a nurse as well as a security guard on board. I worked the trip to coordinate all the details. It seemed like everything was covered.

When we landed in Gatwick, England, we taxied to the terminal and our captain asked Ground Control for fuel. After a little while, a fueling supervisor came on board with a very disturbed look on his face. As it turned out, our flight control people had failed to obtain a credit standing for this fuel company in Europe and they refused to fuel our plane. As luck would have it, I had a credit card for this company with me that I used for my automobile. In the face of a complete disaster with

ITT, I calmly took out my fuel credit card. After studying the back, which contained no credit limit, I handed the card to the fueling supervisor and said, "Fill it up."

The fuel company billed my personal card for thousands of dollars and this saved the day.

208
"The man who views the world at 50 the same as he did at 20 has wasted 30 years of his life."
– Muhammad Ali

209
"The next time you are having a bad day, remember that even gray skies are just clouds passing over."
– Teddy Roosevelt

210
In business, as in life, it's all about phrasing. If you look a woman in the eye and tell her that she can make time stand still, that's one thing. If you tell her that she has a face that could stop a clock, that's another thing entirely.

211

Executives under sixty usually like gifts that are electronic. Executives over sixty usually like anything alcoholic.

212

It takes great skill to make many of your business guests feel at home – especially when you wish they were.

213

The easiest thing to achieve in business with almost no effort is failure ... but success isn't about "easy" is it?

214

Never volunteer to confront the company president with the demands of all the other employees.

215

The next time you complain about your problems remember; if they weren't so difficult, someone with less ability would probably have your job.

216

Worrying about what's right is always more important than worrying about who's right.

217

"Too many times, too many of us, are simply too far removed from the issues to fully assess them. It isn't that we can't find the solution. It's that we can't see the problem."

> – Bob Tillman
> President and CEO
> Lowe's Companies, Inc.

218

Chief executives discuss concepts. Senior executives discuss events. Middle executives discuss people. Non-executives discuss tasks. As a step in moving ahead in corporate life, step up one level in your discussions.

219

Usually the person who is the first to jump up and throw another log on the fire is not the one who had to split the wood in the first place.

Ben Frankly says ...

"A great danger in business is not that you aim too high and miss it ... it is that you aim too low and hit it."

221
Problems that affect everyone
are best solved by everyone.

222
The major difference between a successful person and
one who isn't is usually a lack of confidence to try.

223
Don't let group-think keep you from expressing
your honest thoughts and feelings.

224
"All of our dreams can come true,
if we have the courage to pursue them."
– Walt Disney

225
To succeed, no matter how silly your ideas may
seem, speak up. Remember, the forest would be
very silent if no birds sang except the very best.

226

Don't be afraid to go out on a limb:
that's where the fruit is.

227

An executive too busy to take care of his employees
is like a mechanic too busy to take care of his tools.

228

Profit projections are sometimes similar to the
horizon which is defined as an imaginary line that
disappears as you get closer.

229

Junior executives get ... middle executives improve
... senior executives spend.

230

Dumb executives have a talent for saying the
correct thing at the proper time to the wrong people.

231
Don't make difficult people
the center of your emotional life.

232
Only a mediocre executive is always at his best.

233
Lawyers earn more from problems than solutions.

234
Keeping up is always easier than catching up.

235
God gave us two ears and one mouth
so we could listen twice as much as we talk.

236
"'Broke' can be defined as a temporary situation
... 'Poor' is a state of life."
– Bill Russell

237

Obligations are bankable.

238

Never use push when you've got pull.

239

The true entrepreneur knows that
when life gives you scraps, you make a quilt.

240

ALL SUCCESSFUL BUSINESS BUILDERS LEARN TO THINK OUTSIDE THE BOX

My friend, Mark H. McCormack, the Founder of International Management Group, once wrote:

Business demands innovation. There is a constant need to feel around the fringes, to test the edges, but business schools, out of necessity, are condemned to teach the past. This not only perpetuates conventional thinking; it stifles innovation. I once heard someone say that if Thomas Edison had gone to business school we would all be reading by larger candles.

Sometimes business mirrors life. For example, it doesn't matter how many pails of milk you spill … just don't lose the cow.

242

If something is right, it can be done;
if it's wrong, it can be done without.

243

Agreement in principle
is the politest form of disagreement.

244

REAL LEADERS ARE REMEMBERED
FOR REAL ACCOMPLISHMENTS

My friend, Wally Amos, who founded Famous
Amos cookies and The Uncle Noname Cookie
Company, recently gave me an anecdote he lives by
and is included in his book *Watermelon Magic:
Seeds of Wisdom, Slices of Life*. His anecdote really
gets you thinking about the meaning of life. Each
day all of us work very hard at what we do, but
when it's all over, what will people remember about
us? Here's Wally's quote:

Obituaries always list the year you were
born and the year you died, separated by a
dash, i.e. 1900-1996. When you were born
or when you died is not nearly as important
as what you did in between – what you put
in your dash.

245

Aim at nothing and you can't miss.

246

The conscientious executive arrives early
and leaves when it's over!

247

"Throw strikes. Home plate don't move."
– Satchel Paige

248

A Ferrari doesn't win races ... the driver does.

249

If you want to get ahead at work,
do your job as if you owned the business.

250

Some people dream about fishing and never leave
the dock. Others have learned that the more times
you cast your net into the water, the better your
chances of catching a fish.

251
No matter how thin you slice it,
there are always two sides.

252
"Out of intense complexities
intense simplicities emerge."
– Albert Einstein

253
A smart executive will let difficult times
make him a better person, not a bitter one.

254
"As long as the mind can envision the fact that you
can do something, you can do it."
– Arnold Schwarzenegger

255
To inherit the future one must be constantly learning.
Those who have finished learning will find
themselves well-equipped to live in the past.

256

Leadership is action, not position.

257

Your reputation both precedes and follows you.

258

The reason why worry kills more executives than hard work is that more executives worry than work hard.

259

Leaders are like shepherds. However, if they take credit for everything, they will only frustrate their flock, who will then seek other shepherds in the organization to lead them to their destination.

260

"Now, I'm saying if I've got a goose that can lay a golden egg, then I would study that goose and say 'How can I get it to lay two eggs?' – not, 'Should we have it for Thanksgiving dinner?'"

– Ross Perot

"You are a CEO, you must expect challenges, extreme frustration, tremendous lapses in confidence, even failure … but hey, that's golf, now about your business …"

262

"The truth is always more important than the facts."
– Frank Lloyd Wright

263

Obstacles are things people see
when they stop watching their goal.

264

The more sand that escapes from the hourglass of
an executive's life, the clearer he should see
through it.

265

When traveling abroad, it is best to remember that
money, not English, is the international language.

266

It usually takes as much time to sell a cheap product
as it does to sell an expensive one … the difference
is in the amount of commission earned.

267

"Successful employers seek staff who will do the unusual, who think, and who attract attention by performing more than is expected of them."
– Charles M. Schwab

268

In corporate life it is interesting to observe that senior executives see everything ... middle executives suspect everything ... junior executives know everything.

269

In business today, too many executives spend money they haven't earned, to buy things they don't need, to impress people they don't even like.

270

Anyone can climb the ladder of success, but it's the smart executive who makes sure it's leaning against the right building.

271

"I made a fortune getting out too soon."
– J.P. Morgan

272

If you don't pay attention to your customers, eventually your customers won't pay attention to you.

273

When checking references, always ask: "Would you hire this person again?" Any answer other than "yes" is a "NO."

274

A skilled executive
can hear what was not being said.

275

In business, the level of dissension increases exponentially with an increase in the number of issues management must philosophize over.

276

When nothing seems to help, remember the stonecutter hammering away at his rock perhaps a hundred times without as much as a crack showing. Yet at the hundred and first blow it will split in two. Know it was not the final blow that did it – but all that had gone before.

277

"YOU CANNOT FLY WITH THE EAGLES AND ACT LIKE A CANARY."

Not long ago, I was given a copy of Alan Greenberg's book, *Memos From The Chairman*. Alan is the chairman of Bear Stearns Companies and his book is something that everyone in business should read. One day when we were speaking, I asked Alan for a personal anecdote for my book and he faxed me the following:

> Some years ago the bond market dropped considerably. A business reporter from one of the newspapers called me and said they knew Bear Stearns is active in bonds and did we lose any money because of the decline? I told him you cannot fly with the eagles and act like a canary. I believe that.

"I come here on weekends so Mondays don't completely overwhelm me."

279

INTEGRITY AND EXCELLENCE EQUAL SUCCESS

The most exciting time in my entire business career occurred during my years with American Airlines. I had the privilege of working with C. R. Smith, the founder, and in those early days I couldn't wait to get to work. On most days, I worked from 12 to 14 hours a day in an atmosphere charged with energy.

A few years after I started, the company hired a new CFO named Robert Crandall. Bob certainly fit the company profile – he had more energy than anyone I had ever met and did not understand the meaning of "can't do that" – it just wasn't in his vocabulary – and people quickly learned it should not be in theirs, either.

Bob quickly moved into the top marketing spot and ultimately advanced to chairman of AMR Corporation/American Airlines. We have been friends for over 30 years and my respect for him, both as an individual and a businessman, has never wavered. He sent me the following inclusion for this book and it is so essentially "Bob Crandall." It is why he moved forward to become chairman of American, and such valuable advice for anyone who wants to achieve success that I am proud to share it with you:

> Two of the most important qualities of an outstanding leader are integrity – to say what you mean, to deliver what you promise and to stand for what is right – and excellence – to be satisfied with no performance short of the best.

280
If your work ends at five, it's a job.
If it goes beyond that time, it's a career.

281
An equal partner should not be someone who brings potential to a venture but someone who stands to lose as much as you when things go wrong.

282
Most of the time the trip is more exciting than the destination.

283
The wise executive can make stumbling blocks into stepping stones.

284

Common sense and consistency will succeed more frequently than raw genius.

285

What you are always speaks louder than
what you say.

286

There are two types of fools:
Those who trust everyone and those who trust no one.

287

Anyone who accepts "good enough" as their work standard should know that such a standard isn't good enough at all.

288

The greatest thing about the future is that it comes along day by day and allows us the time to influence its outcome.

289

Doing the right thing is always more important
than doing things right.

290

Nothing is a greater impediment to being on good
terms with others than being ill at ease with yourself.

291

The more interesting the gossip,
the more likely it is to be untrue.

292

If your company is stupid enough to be run by a
committee, be on that committee.

293

The bitterness of poor quality remains long after
the sweetness of meeting the schedule has been
forgotten.

Don't hold a $1,000 meeting
to solve a $100 problem!

295

The beginning is half of every action.

296

You can't control your heritage,
but you can control your future.

297

People who will lie for you will lie to you.

298

Just because you don't get paid more than a baseball
player, it doesn't mean you're not as important.

299

No single job has a future. Only you have a future.

300

Some people spend so much time talking about what
they have to do that they don't have enough time to
do anything.

301
Never get drunk with strangers.

302
"It's not whether you get knocked down.
It's whether you get up again."
– Vince Lombardi
Former NFL Coach

303
In business it's always easier to stay out of trouble
than to get out of trouble.

304
Don't try to do something cheaply
that shouldn't be done at all.

305
"The value of a man should be seen in what he
gives and not in what he is able to receive."
– Albert Einstein

306

Half-finished work is labor lost.

307

It's not great ideas that succeed,
it's great people who make them succeed.

308

Only make a great deal if you have no intention of
ever doing business with that person again.
Otherwise, make a good deal.

309

INITIATE, FOLLOW UP, THANK, AND SUCCEED

A friend of mine, Mort Naiman, who was a director
for the Jewish National Fund, shared something
with me that I also strongly agree with:

> I have found that people who do not wait
> for things to happen but initiate them;
> who stay on top or follow up as a rule;
> who give proper acknowledgment or
> thanks; are usually successful in whatever
> they do.

310
Nothing will ever be attempted,
if all possible objections must be overcome.

311
In business, a man should not be judged by what he eats so much as with whom he eats.

312
"A little humility makes you perfect."
– Ted Turner

313
"I don't know the key to success, but the key to failure is trying to please everybody."
– Bill Cosby

314
Companies that are downsizing should remember that age is important only if you are cheese – integrity, ability and performance are the true measurement of importance.

Ben Frankly says ...

"It seems like years ago business executives were afraid because they did not have all the facts ... today, they're afraid because they do."

316

The executive who makes no mistakes
usually doesn't make anything.

317

The concerned investment banker is the one who
blows the horn on his Mercedes as he drives
through a red light.

318

To drive your business to success, try to view
opportunities through the front windshield and not
in the rearview mirror.

319

Having something to say is always more important
than wanting to say something.

320

Sometimes, when a man with money meets a man
with experience, the man with experience ends up
with the money and the man with the money ends
up with experience.

321
Even the mighty oak was once a nut.

322
Goals without time limits are called wishes ...
some even call them dreams.

323
At your child's college graduation you'll never say
that you wish you'd spent more time working.

324
The reason most executives speak about the past is
that it is easier to remember where they've been
than to figure out where they're going.

325
All junior executives should know that if they work
hard ten hours a day, every day, they could be
promoted to senior executives so that they can work
hard for fourteen hours a day.

326
THE TEN COMMANDMENTS OF STREET SMARTS
BY MARK H. MCCORMACK

1. Never underestimate the importance of money ...
   it's how business people keep score!

2. Never overestimate the value of money ...
   Cash is important, but sometimes not as important
   as respect, thanks, integrity, or the thrill of a job
   well-done.

3. You can never have too many friends in business ...
   Given a choice, always do business with a friend.
   It's the best way to leverage your success.

4. Don't be afraid to say, "I don't know" ...
   People will respect you much more and will always
   place more weight on what you do say, because
   they know you're right.

5. Speak less ...
   No one ever put their foot in their mouth when they
   were *not* speaking. Worse, if you are speaking, you
   can't be listening and we always learn much more
   from listening.

6. Keep your promises, the big ones and the little ones ...
   Both the starting point and the staying point in any
   business relationship is trust, not suspicion. Someone

who does what he says he will do will always succeed over a person who doesn't keep his word.

7. Every transaction has a life of its own ...
   Some need tender loving care, some need to be hurried away.

8. Commit yourself to quality from day one ...
   It's better to do nothing at all than to do something badly.

9. Be nice to people ...
   Nice gets nice, and all things being equal, courtesy can be very persuasive.

10. Don't hog the credit, share it ...
    People will work with you and for you if they are recognized. They will also work against you if they are not.

Author's Note:
Mark McCormack founded International Management Group (IMG) in 1960, and I have worked with him in a variety of transactions since 1979. Mark built IMG into the world's leading organization in the field of athlete representation and sports marketing.

If you know how, you will always have a job.
If you know why, you'll be the boss.

328

Try not to work in the same office
as someone you once slept with.

329

Dumb executives tend to become best friends with
other dumb executives.

330

"You never get ahead of anyone
as long as you try to get even with him."
– Lou Holtz

331

Those who have the most demanding bosses are
those who are self-employed.

332

If you wait for opportunity to emerge, all your
competitors will be there to help you take advantage of
it. If you can find opportunities before they emerge,
your competitors will be forced to follow you.

333
If you don't keep doing it better,
a competitor will.

334
A goal is important. If you don't know where you are going, chances are you'll miss it when you get there.

335
"There are two times in a man's life when he should not speculate – when he cannot afford it, and when he can."

– Mark Twain

336
"I'm sort of like the old fellow standing by the side of the road. A Cadillac pulled up and the driver asked him if he knew where New Boston was. The old fellow answered, 'No.' The driver asked if he knew where Gladewater was, and the old man said he didn't. The driver then said, 'What in the world do you know?' The old fellow answered, 'I know I'm not lost.'"

– Ross Perot

337

Smart executives retire from something
to something.

338

Senior executives can't help getting older,
but they certainly don't have to act older.

339

An army of lions led by a sheep will always be
defeated by an army of sheep led by a lion.

340

Always try to do the right thing, unless your
conscience tells you otherwise.

341

If you wish to build a successful company, hire
wonderful employees. But remember, employees
are like house plants. They require regular care or
they will not last.

342

When measuring someone's ethics, remember, behavior is always more telling than conversation.

343

One must never be satisfied doing only what one can; one must always do what one really cannot.

344

The primary benefit of a sharp tongue is that you've always got something handy to cut your own throat.

345

The value of a retiring executive should not be measured by his length of service but by his quality of performance.

346

When considering a promotion, remember that the difference between an ordinary employee and the extraordinary one is "extra." Most promotions go to the employee who understands that.

Sometimes business is like a battle. Remember the words of General George Patton: "If you go into battle, it's better to win the first time."

348

To get the right answer,
it helps to ask the right question.

349

Most customers vote with their checkbooks whether
or not you will stay in business.

350

A deal that doesn't close right away
usually never does.

351

"Plans are nothing – planning is everything."
– Dwight D. Eisenhower

352

"When one door closes, another opens; but we often
look so long and so regretfully upon the closed door
that we do not see the one which has opened for us."
– Alexander Graham Bell

353
There are no shortcuts
to any destination worth going to.

354
In business, as in life, imaginary difficulties are harder to overcome than real ones.

355
Most of the time it is important to get a return on your money. Sometimes it's important to just get a return *of* your money.

356
Always remember that most significant achievements were once considered impossible.

357
When your head and your heart are moving in the right direction, chances are your feet are moving in that direction, too.

358

Once solved, all problems are simple.

359

IT TAKES GREAT PEOPLE
TO BUILD A GREAT BUSINESS

A person I respect very much is Eileen Ford. She created one of the most successful modeling agencies in the world and launched hundreds of young people into fame and fortune. Eileen was a neighbor and once told me how much she liked the snacks that Greenfield Healthy Foods made. (This is the company I founded and later sold to Campbell Soup). It gave me the opportunity to ask her thoughts about success. She told me:

> I believe success in business is directly related to the quality and character of your staff. I couldn't have built Ford Models, Inc. without the support of my exceptional co-workers. I would counsel anyone reading John's book to pay particular care in selecting the right people to help you achieve success. In fact, I took so much care that I married my single most important co-worker. I consider myself very blessed to have been able to work with my husband, Jerry, and I know Ford Models wouldn't be the success it is today without him.

360

The smart executive knows all the rules
so he can break them wisely.

361

Successful executives know that when opportunity
doesn't knock, they should open the door anyway.

362

The best way to eliminate any enemy
is to make him a friend.

363

"You make more friends by becoming interested in
other people than by trying to interest other people
in yourself."
– Dale Carnegie

364

Operating a business with no advertising is like
winking at a beautiful woman in the dark ... you
know what you're doing, but nobody else does.

365

Ben Frankly says ...

"I used to complain about my job until I thought about not having it."

366

"If you don't think too good,
then don't think too much."
– Ted Williams

367

People who are satisfied with their current position
will probably stay there. But those who really
believe they can do better will always move ahead.

368

"Destiny is not a matter of chance;
it is a matter of choice."
– William Jennings Bryan

369

Loyalty bought with money
can always be overcome with money.

370

Special interests are called "special" because they
have no interest in the general interest.

371

Quality represents the wisest choice
of many alternatives.

372

Executives who make a big deal about being right should remember that even a broken clock is right twice a day.

373

"Aerodynamically the bumble bee shouldn't be able to fly, but the bumble bee doesn't know it, so it goes on flying anyway."
– Mary Kay Ash

374

Visit your top fifty customers at least once a year.

375

Be an executive who says: "It may be difficult, but it's possible" … not one who says: "It may be possible, but it's too difficult."

EFFORT GETS EFFORT

I receive about ten unsolicited résumés every month from people looking for jobs. They all have the same sort of cover letters – something like: "Are you looking for a bright person who increased sales in his last company by 300%?" I always wonder, if this guy's so bright and brought in all that new business, why is he out of a job?

I would like to ask whoever is helping all these people to start giving them some real world advice:

1. Knock off the hype in the cover letter.

2. Do your homework. Make every letter count. Take a rifle shot not the shotgun approach. Find out everything about the prospect company. What do they do? What do they make? Who runs the company? Where are the offices? What are their problems? Who's their competition?

3. Now write a cover letter that is designed to specifically fit the company and a particular job. Show the reader you think enough of his or her company (and their time) to have done your homework. I will read a letter from someone who took the time to research my business, and if we don't have a position, I will even send the letter to someone I think could use this person's talents. Effort gets effort.

377
Avoid debt.

378
Using only market research to make decisions is like driving a car using a rearview mirror.

379
You qualify as a Type "A" personality if you stoop to tie your shoe and wonder what else you can do while you're down there.

380
Never lend money to your boss.

381
"When the pace of change outside an organization becomes greater than the pace of change inside the organization, the end is near."
— John R. Walter
Former President
AT&T

Sometimes, it's just about semantics.

383
Nothing Is Impossible

A number of years ago, we sold our snack food company to the Campbell Soup Company. I stayed on as a consultant for a few years and one of the ways I felt we could expand our sales was to establish the line as a "cult" product with a strong celebrity following. I interviewed several promotion and public relations companies who quoted me hundreds of thousands of dollars to simply get a few top celebrities to "try" our products. It would then cost hundreds of thousands of additional dollars to actually get them to endorse the products. Given the expense, I decided to put the celebrity campaign on the back burner.

That summer I took my high school aged son to California to visit UCLA and USC. As we drove from the Beverly Hilton Hotel to UCLA on Sunset Boulevard, we passed a hand-painted sign that said "Star Maps for Sale, Next Right." I immediately told my son to slow down and make the next right. Sure enough, there was a young boy sitting on a milk crate selling maps which identified the residences of hundreds of the top movie stars for $7.50. I bought a map.

When we returned home, I asked one of our staff to take on an assignment. We wrote a personal letter to over 100 superstars and sent it to their homes with a complimentary box of products and asked them for their comments. Only one star refused the shipment. We received 32 great letters of support. Several celebrities even asked for monthly shipments. We compiled all of the wonderful letters into a book and utilized it in our sales presentations to supermarket buyers. I estimated the project would have cost us about $750,000 if we had gone about doing it the conventional way, not $7.50, the unconventional way.

384
If you lie down in the face of conflict,
someone will surely walk over you.

385
Many senior executives spend the second half of their lives recovering from the first half.

386
The future belongs to the learned,
not to the historian.

QUESTION ENOUGH
AND YOU WILL FIND THE ANSWER

I was playing squash the other night with my colleague Ted Giannitti, and he told me the amazing story of Stanislavsky Lech who saved his own life by constantly questioning until he found the answer.

Stanislavsky and his family were arrested by the Nazis during World War II and sent to a death camp in Krakow. His entire family was shot in front of him and he was forced into hard labor.

Starving to death he somehow continued, knowing that if he didn't escape he would surely die. He questioned how to survive every minute of every day. His friends told him it was useless and that he should simply pray; but he refused to accept this and continued to question, continued to search for a solution.

Finally, the solution presented itself. The Germans would pile bodies next to the gas chambers and each day load them into trucks to be dumped into mass graves.

As his work day ended, Lech slipped out of line, ducked behind a truck loaded with bodies, removed his clothing and, while no one was looking, jumped into the back of the truck with the dead. More bodies were dumped on top of him and he lay quiet, pretending to be dead.

Finally, the truck moved outside the camp gravesite and dumped the bodies. Lech stayed silent for hours until dark and then ran naked over 25 miles to freedom.

Why did Lech survive? Because he refused to give up. More important, he had continued questioning until he found a solution.

In business, if something isn't right, we have two choices: accept it or question it to find a solution. Sometimes you have to ask many questions to find the right answer. The key is to never stop questioning until you are satisfied with the answer.

388
Success is a journey,
not a destination.

389
If you can't do great things every day,
at least do small things in a great way.

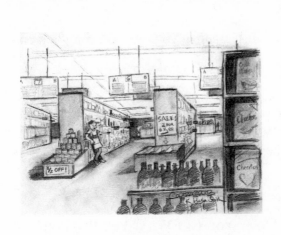

If you don't think the customer is
important, try going without him
for 30 days.

391

Fear of becoming a failure
keeps weak executives from becoming anything.

392

Nothing less than your best is even good enough.

393

Happiness and excellence are directly related.
Knowing how to do your job well is directly related
to how much you will enjoy doing it.

394

YOU GET WHAT YOU PAY FOR

A popular story within the cruise line industry
relates that on April 12, 1912, a British citizen, Mr. Ralph
Hendersen, successfully argued that he shouldn't
have to pay the full rate for his outside cabin on his
cruise ship. Hendersen pointed out that the ship
was new and its crew was still learning the various
service routines of the ship. Reluctantly, he was
given a 10% discount by the reservations manager of
the H.M.S. Titanic.

395

Life is something that happens to you
while you are making other plans.

396

THE HIGHER THE PRICE
THE BETTER THE QUALITY

Why do consumers believe this? I've always been
amazed that when confronted with two very similar
products, many consumers will purchase the more
expensive one.

Why? Because it must be of a higher quality? This
isn't always true.

I remember when I was in high school and working
afternoons at a small upscale grocery market. One
of my responsibilities was to go directly across the
street to our local A&P and purchase a few dozen
apples at 5¢ each, bring them back to our market,
polish them and stack them very neatly in the front
of our store. We sold them for 25¢ each and we
sold out every day.

Why? Because at 25¢, everyone in town believed
we had the very best apples available.

397

Allow an extra two weeks for every deadline.

398

Extremely successful executives should know that those moments which are absolutely free from worry are called panic.

399

In contract law a completion date should be defined as the point at which liquidated damages begin.

400

Successful executives have learned to pay more attention to what employees actually do rather than to what they say they'll do.

401

DON'T EVER UNDERESTIMATE YOUR CUSTOMER
Consumers are really very smart. When you reduce the quality of your product to save a buck they really do notice ... and usually they also save a buck ... they stop buying your product.

402

Get the whole story before making a decision.

403

Be sure your handwriting is easily deciphered.

404

If you are ill at ease when speaking, practice. If you are comfortable speaking, practice.

405

Seek and publicize testimonials.

406

BEEN THERE, DONE THAT

I have known Gerry Roche, the chairman of Heidrick & Struggles for more than a decade. Gerry heads up one of the best executive search firms in the world and once gave me a maxim that makes great sense:

"You can no more tell somebody to do something that you ain't done, than you can come back from someplace where you ain't been."

"I'm afraid our CFO, Mr. Huntington,
will be away from the office for a while.
May I take a message?"

408

It is never too late
to become what you might have become.

409

The most important thing that keeps most people
from becoming successful is hard work.

410

**MORE PEOPLE GET INTO TROUBLE FOR THINGS
THEY SAY RATHER THAN FOR WHAT THEY DO**

General Westmoreland called down to the base
motor pool one day and asked what vehicles were
on the base and available. The Private who
answered the call said: "Two jeeps, one truck, and
one sedan for the stupid General." Not believing
what he just heard, the General asked the Private:
"Do you know who you're talking to?" The Private
said: "No." "Well, this is General Westmoreland."
The Private thought for a moment – highly aware of
his incredible blunder -- and asked: "Well, do you
know who you're talking to?" The General
responded "No, I don't," to which the Private said:
"Well, so long, stupid" and hung up the phone.

411
Lead, follow, or get out of the way.

412
Ninety percent of the time things will turn out worse than you expect. The other ten percent of the time you had no right to expect so much.

413
TO SURVIVE IN BUSINESS YOU MUST BE ABLE TO THINK AND ACT QUICKLY

A story circulated around Wall Street a while ago about a tough chairman of a major company who stopped into the famous restaurant "21" for a quick bite. Not being too hungry, he asked the waiter for half of a sirloin steak. Normally the waiter would simply have told him they didn't serve half-steaks, but given the importance of this customer, the waiter agreed and left for the kitchen. Unbeknownst to the waiter, the chairman followed him to the kitchen to tell him he wanted the steak rare. As the waiter announced to the chef, "I need half a steak for a real jerk," he noticed the chairman standing behind him and, without missing a beat, continued to comment to the chef, "and the other half goes to this gentleman."

414

THE RACE TO SUCCESS HAS NO FINISH LINE

You can usually pick those companies with exceptional leadership simply by observing the quality of their products or service.

Victor H. Doolan, the former president of BMW, participated in my first book several years ago and he gave me one of his personal success maxims that I wanted to share in this book: "For us there is no finish line."

As a very long-time BMW customer I can honestly tell you that this company has no finish line ... every year their product gets better and better.

Victor Doolan represents the poster child for any leader that strives for excellence. His attitude kept BMW at the leading edge and his philosophy of "no finish line" is one of the best maxims any CEO can share with his or her fellow employees.

Victor is now the president at Volvo and I am sure you will continue to see Volvo also produce finer and finer vehicles.

415
Never act out of malice.

416
NECESSITY IS THE MOTHER OF INVENTION

Twenty years ago, we moved to a home located in a large wooded area in Connecticut. One morning I spotted a man walking around the side of our house. Thinking he was a prowler, I approached the man slowly with my .38 cal handgun. As it turned out, I almost shot the electric company meter reader. So I decided to buy a device that I could put at the beginning of my driveway that would alert me if someone was coming. I found that the only sensors available required a wire to be run underground from the end of the driveway to the house. Since my driveway was about $1/4$ mile long, the cost to install a system was $2,500. I saw an opportunity and hired an electrical engineer to make me a prototype of a radio-operated driveway detector. Once we had perfected the prototype, I formed a company to market driveway detectors and struck a contract with a major alarm manufacturer to produce our products. After the first year, we had sales in the hundreds of thousands of dollars and I sold the company for a wonderful profit.

Ben Frankly says ...

"Why is it that some experts are smart enough to tell you how to run your business, but not smart enough to start their own?"

418
Empower the people around you to win, and they will make you a winner.

419
The meek might inherit the earth, but the strong will always retain the mineral rights.

420
The critical path method is a management technique for losing your shirt under perfect control.

421
Where you are is important, but not as important as where you are going.

422
THERE ARE ALWAYS TWO SIDES TO EVERY STORY
When asked his opinion on a play that did not receive great reviews, Oscar Wilde, the famous British writer, once commented: "The play was wonderful ... the audience was a disaster."

423

If a sufficient number of management layers are stacked on top of each other, it can be assured that disaster is not left to chance.

424

YOU RARELY GET INTO TROUBLE WHEN YOU KEEP YOUR MOUTH SHUT

More people in business get into trouble for saying the wrong thing to the wrong people at the wrong time. There's a great Mark Twain tale that makes this point.

Mark once spent three weeks in Maine fishing during the closed season. On his return to New York in the lounge car of the train, with his illegal catch on ice in the baggage car, he struck up a conversation with a stranger to relate the story of his successful fishing exploit. The stranger's expression grew more grim with each of Twain's boasts. Finally, Twain asked: "By the way, who are you?" "I'm the State Game Warden," was the unwelcome reply, "and who are you?" Twain, nearly white with fright, answered: "Well, to be totally truthful, Warden, I'm the biggest damned liar in the whole United States."

425
Negotiation At Its Best
J.P. Morgan was interested in buying a pearl pin. The jeweler he approached found the perfect pin and sent it in a box to Morgan with a bill for $5,000. The following day the box was returned with a note from Morgan: "I like the pin, but I don't like the price. If you will accept the enclosed check for $4,000, please send back the box which is sealed with the seal unbroken." The enraged jeweler returned the check to the messenger and dismissed him in anger. He opened the box to remove the pin only to find that it had already been replaced with a check from Morgan for $5,000.

426
"Don't build me a watch, just tell me the time."
– Charlie McCarthy
    Former Chief Operating Officer
    Tetley USA

427
"Farming looks mighty easy when your plow is a pencil and you're a thousand miles from the corn field."
– Dwight D. Eisenhower

428
Decisions reduce anxiety.

429
The wise executive never shoots a messenger bringing bad news because, after a while, all he'll receive is the good news.

430
LEADERS MUST BE GOOD COMMUNICATORS
Most of the world's finest and most successful companies are run by leaders who understand the value of good communication. Leaders who never leave their office – who never communicate with their organizations – will never see their companies achieve their maximum potential.

Ron Allen, the former chairman, president, and CEO of Delta Air Lines gave me one of his observations on the value of good communications and it is so correct that I would like to share it with you:

"Leaders must be good communicators. However, it is always easier to lead when your organization is already going in the same direction that you are."

A turn in the road is not the end of the road … unless you fail to make the turn.

432

Nothing is more rewarding than to watch someone who says it can't be done get interrupted by someone actually doing it.

433

"If your time is too precious to give to your friends or family – change your lifestyle."
– Peter Capozzi

434

"If you're right, you just hang in there, stand your ground and don't give an inch. If you have the will to do that, at some point the tide will turn."
– Ross Perot

435
THE TRUTH BE KNOWN!

At a political dinner the famous newspaper columnist, Ann Landers, was introduced to a rather pompous Senator. "So, you're Ann Landers," he drawled. "Say something funny." Without hesitation Ann replied: "Well, you're a politician ... tell me a lie."

THE POWER OF POSITIVE THINKING

Nothing upsets me more than an employee who immediately starts telling me why something won't work. If we spend two hours in a meeting discussing why something won't work, that's two hours we could have spent trying to identify how to make something work. The good manager will be alert to negative thinkers and will build positive responses to move negative employees back on track.

For example, when someone says: "We've never done that before," you answer: "We have a great opportunity to be first." "We already tried that," can be answered with: "What did we learn from our previous experience that will allow us to try again?" "We'll cannibalize our existing sales," should be answered with: "Let's increase our business and develop programs to protect against cannibalization." "We don't have the expertise," should be answered with: "Let's find the expertise to make this work." "Our customers won't go for it," should be answered with: "Let's show our customers some new opportunities." "Our product is good enough," should be countered with: "Let's try to improve our product before our competition does."

In my experience negative thinkers drive negative bottom lines. Businesses are built with positive thinkers.

437

"If it looks like a duck, walks like a duck, and quacks like a duck, chances are it's a duck."
— Senator Edward Kennedy

438

If someone says something unkind about you, live your life so that no one will believe it.

439

The exceptional manager will always expect that the expected can be prevented, and that the unexpected should have been expected.

440

An executive who can't forget is much worse than one who can't remember.

441

"Pressure is when you've got thirty-five bucks riding on a four-foot putt and you've only got five dollars."
— Lee Trevino

442

A union strike is like trying to increase the egg production by strangling the chicken.

443
TAKE RISKS

A few years ago, I had dinner with Jim Burke. We were supporting a "One to One" function for our mutual friend, Ray Chambers, and we got into a discussion about taking risks in business. Jim told me a wonderful story that I would like to share with you:

Jim Burke became the head of a new products group at Johnson & Johnson. One of his first products was a children's chest rub. It failed miserably and Jim believed he would be fired when he was called into the Chairman's office. However, to his surprise, after Mr. Johnson asked if he was the one who just cost the company a lot of money he then added, "Well, I want to congratulate you. If you made a mistake it means you took a risk, and if we don't take risks we will never grow. That is what business is all about." Years later Jim Burke became the chairman of Johnson & Johnson.

People who are constantly looking into
the past are unlikely to see the hole up ahead.

445

Never let what you can't do
interfere with what you can do.

446

Remember, in business, committees may keep
minutes ... but they usually cost the company hours.

447

There is very little difference between most
executives ... but that little difference makes a very
big difference. The little difference is attitude. The
big difference is whether it is positive or negative.

448

All good things come to him who waits ...
as long as he works like hell while he waits.

449

Everyone is surrounded by opportunities, but they
only exist once they have been seen. They will only
be seen if they are looked for, and they will only be
looked for if you have a goal to achieve.

NEVER DO OR SAY SOMETHING TO SOMEONE THAT YOU WOULD NOT WANT THEM TO DO OR SAY TO YOU

Many years ago, I sat next to Dom Rossi in an airplane from Detroit to New York. At that time, he was president of N.W. Ayer, the oldest and one of the largest advertising agencies in the world. We have become "brothers" over the years. Our kids went to the same school, we belong to the same church, he was an owner in several of my companies and sat on one of my boards. I respect him very much. The above maxim is one I have taught my children all their lives and I am honored to know it is a maxim in which Dom also believes. He sent me the following anecdote and if everyone in business lived by it, the world would be a much better place. He said:

A long time ago, I was sitting at a recreation league basketball game with a group of teenage friends. There was an elderly janitor sweeping the area adjacent to the court, and several of the kids started to call him names and have fun at his expense.

I asked one of the kids if he would be doing this if the man who was the target of their insensitive behavior was his grandfather. He responded quickly, "Of course not!" stopped, thought for a moment about what he just said, and told his friends to stop. They did.

My mom taught me the above maxim when I was a young boy and I have followed it carefully throughout my entire business career. I know it has served me well, and I hope everyone who reads this book stops for a moment, like my teenage friend did at our basketball game, to reflect on their interpersonal skills which are so important if one wishes to succeed in business today.

451
People who strike out at someone when they get angry should be careful not to strike themselves.

452
All who snore are not always sleeping.

453
In any new business, overvalue the negative projections by two. Undervalue the positive projections by half.

454

Any man who wants to hang himself
can always find a noose.

455

In business, as in fishing,
trouble starts when you open your mouth.

456

Eagles don't hunt flies.

457

If you're skating on thin ice, skate real fast.

458

Old wolves may lose their teeth
but never their nature.

459

You know you are working too hard when you get
all excited because it's Saturday and you can wear
your sweats to work.

Ben Frankly says ...

"The problem with success is that by the time you're rich enough to sleep late, you're old enough so that you always wake up early."

461
To finish sooner, take your time.

462
Act like a jerk and people will think that you are.

463
Working hard to succeed is always better than working a little to fail.

464
"THE LESS BAGGAGE ... THE EASIER THE RIDE." My friend, Wally Amos, once said: "My experiences have shown me that life truly is a journey, and the less baggage we carry the easier the ride."

I also define baggage as doing business with people you don't like, don't trust, or just find annoying. Clearly, that isn't always possible, but consider how great it would be to go through a day only speaking to people you truly enjoy.

A goal should be to try to cut back on anything negative so all you have left are the positives.

Solve The Objection To Make A Sale

A few years ago, a good friend asked me to help his son who owned a pet store that wasn't doing very well. The boy sold the usual dogs, cats, fish, turtles, pet food, and miscellaneous related supplies. At first I resisted getting involved since I didn't have a background in pet retailing and I also felt that if the boy went out of business after I gave him my advice, I would probably lose my friendship with his father.

Since this was a good friend, my desire to help won out over my better judgment. I went down to the store and met with the boy. The location was okay, it could have been better, but to upgrade is a function of available expense dollars which he didn't have. He was just about breaking even.

I reviewed each of his revenue categories and stopped at fish. He had a lot of inventory dollars tied up in fish, tanks, filters, food and the like. He told me he was going to discontinue selling fish because it wasn't making money and the upkeep (cleaning the tanks) was too time consuming. I thought about it for a minute and asked him what he thought the biggest customer objection was to buying pet fish. "Cleaning the tank" was the instant reply.

In sales you must always solve the prospect's objections before making a sale. Based on this premise, I developed a plan.

My suggestion was to produce an inexpensive direct mail brochure which highlighted all the obvious and not-so-obvious benefits of having pet fish. It was not directed to the general public, but to professional and business prospects like doctors, lawyers, clothing stores, restaurants, and other locations that had either a waiting room or lots of public traffic. The key to the new program was to rent the fish and the tanks by the month and, most important, come in each week to clean the tank for a fee. If a fish died, we would replace it at no cost.

Over the next three months alone we signed 42 rental contracts, and established enough cleaning revenue ($20 per week) to cover almost the entire annual rent of the pet store.

Most important, hundreds of people saw the store name on fish tanks all around the area and the publicity generated tremendous exposure and new sales for the store.

466

"We first make our habits,
and then our habits make us."
– John Dryden

467

Learn to profit from your mistakes.
If you can't, your competition will.

468

Making a living should never be confused
with making a life.

469

Man is not the creature of circumstances.
Circumstances are the creatures of man.

470

"Experience is not what happens to a man;
it is what a man does with what happens to him."
– Aldous Huxley

If your only choice is to hire either a conceited executive or a foolish executive, hire the conceited one – occasionally he won't be conceited.

You Can Get Anyone On The Phone
If You Level The Playing Field

Getting an executive who doesn't know you to take your call is always tough. However, all executives are basically the same as you are; they get up in the morning, get dressed, go to the office, and then do whatever it is they do for a living.

The trick to getting past their secretary is to communicate on the same interest level or status level as the executive you are trying to reach. The president of one company is more likely to take a call from the president of another company than from its sales manager.

The sales manager would have a better chance of getting through to another president if his president directed him to make the call and the sales manager mentioned this to the secretary of the executive he is trying to reach.

Interest works the same way, if you know that the president of a company has a particular interest such as stamp collecting and you have a rare stamp to sell, you would probably get through since you are operating on the same interest level.

I once made a completely cold call to the White House and got the President of the United States to take my call. I had purchased an option on the property next door to one of his homes. As his new neighbor, he took my call. I told him I was interested in selling the option and thought he might like to suggest a friend. As it turned out, he gave me several names and I flipped my option on the property to one of the people on his list for a substantial profit.

473

To be very successful, hold yourself to a higher standard than your boss expects of you.

474

"If we did all the things we are capable of doing, we would literally astound ourselves."
– Thomas Edison

475

"Be more concerned with your character than your reputation, because your character is what you really are, while your reputation is merely what others think you are."
– John Wooden

476

Measure twice, cut once.

477

"If you have tried to do something but couldn't, you are far better off than if you had tried to do nothing and succeeded."

– John T. Ragland, Jr.

478

Wealth is a by-product of a man's ability to think.

479

The tiny point of a quick pen
is the sharpest weapon known to man.

480

"We act as though comfort and luxury were the chief requirements of life, when all that we need to be really happy is something to be enthusiastic about."

– Charles Kingsley

481
Take care of your customers
or your competition will.

482
Eat in the company cafeteria at least once a week.

483
"When given a choice ... take both."
– Peter Rogers
Former Chairman
Nabisco Foods

484
The race is not always won by the fastest runner but
sometimes by those who just keep running.

485
"A leader is best when people barely know that he
leads. Not so good when people obey and acclaim
him. Worst when they despise him ... but a good
leader, when his work is done, his aim fulfilled,
they will all say, 'We did this ourselves.'"
– Lao-tzu

Ben Frankly says ...

"If you think you can, you can.
And if you think you can't, you're right."

487

Experience is a good teacher
but she sends terrific bills.

488

If you must do it by the book, be the author.

489

We can't all be executives.
Someone has to actually do the work.

490

It is always better to make payroll
than to collect a paycheck.

491

You can't shake hands with a clenched fist.

492

If your business isn't moving fast enough consider
the turtle ... it can't move at all if it doesn't stick its
neck out.

493

Aim for the top ...
there's more room there.

494

Make sure that the cost of the insurance doesn't exceed the cost of the accident.

495

IF YOU DON'T ASK, YOU DON'T GET

It seems there was a pretzel stand out in front of an office building in New York. One day a man came out of the building, plunked down a quarter, and then went on his way without taking a pretzel. This happened every day for three weeks. Finally, the old lady running the stand spoke up: "Sir, excuse me, may I have a word with you?" The fellow said: "I know what you're going to say. You're going to ask me why I give you a quarter every day and don't take a pretzel." The woman said: "Not at all. I just want to tell you the price is now 35 cents."

> – William Schreyer
> Former Chairman
> Merrill Lynch

496
RESPECT YOUR EMPLOYEES
AND THEY WILL RESPECT YOUR BUSINESS

Some people get it right most of the time and others don't even have a clue. Dick Fogarty, former chairman and CEO of Labatt USA, is one who really understands building a business. He was up to see me awhile ago and told me the following:

> When I was younger and new to the business world, I was totally impatient with idle chatter and anything that got in the way of moving the business forward. At that time, I was somewhat taken back by my division head occasionally *walking the floor* to chat with everyone from the mailroom clerk to the senior managers, and it usually wasn't about business! It was a friendly hello, a pat on the back, a word of encouragement, or perhaps something about the family. It seemed like wasted time to me, but eventually I figured it out. It was all about care, recognition and respect; it was all about running a business well. Executives who don't understand that their employees are their greatest asset will never achieve their maximum success.

As an aside to the above, I was told a story about the principal of Columbus Magnet School in Norwalk, who sat and had lunch every day with an individual student, doing just what Dick Fogarty did. Columbus was voted the best grade school in Connecticut.

497
In any battle,
the best armor is to keep out of range.

498
The truly happy person is the one who can enjoy the scenery even when he must take a detour.

499
If you are in business and have intelligence you don't need to have much else; if you don't have intelligence, it doesn't matter what else you have.

500
Great leadership is the ability to get employees to do what they don't want to do and like doing it.

501
Executives who take cold showers in the morning start the day much more alert. They are also incredible jerks.

Ben Frankly says ...

"Try not to work for a person
who has more problems than you do."

503

"WORRY ABOUT THE SMALL THINGS ... THE BIG THINGS WILL TAKE CARE OF THEMSELVES."

At the beginning of my career, Mr. C.R. Smith, the founder of American Airlines, gave me the above maxim. I was working at LaGuardia Airport on Christmas morning and Mr. Smith came out to thank everyone for working on the holiday. I wonder how many senior executives would do that today?

I have tried to live my business career following Mr. Smith's maxim, and it seems my biggest problems always occur when I don't adhere to it.

Not long ago, my wife and I held a party at our home to honor our friend Michael Bolton for the work he is doing helping high-risk, inner-city children. The Governor issued a special proclamation to recognize Michael and our Mayor presented him with a "Key to the City." We had almost 60 corporate presidents and their spouses attending. I took care of all the "big" things: great caterer, a valet service to park cars and, given the level of importance of all our guests, security guards both in and out of uniform. One uniformed police officer was stationed at the front gate with a guest list to check-in guests as they arrived ... and then a "small thing" happened. Since the party was honoring Michael Bolton, I didn't list him on the guard's guest list. When Michael arrived, the guard would not let him in. The house is almost a $1/4$ mile from the end of the driveway so there was no way I could know what was going on. Fortunately, Michael is one of the more resourceful people I know and he convinced the guard he really was invited to "his" party and was let in.

504
"Some men see things and say 'why?' I dream of things that never were and ask, 'why not?'"
– John F. Kennedy

505
"Business is like dogsledding. If you are not the lead dog, your view will always be the same."
– Bernal Quiros

506
Remember to dig deep when interviewing someone for a key position. Just as a wise man can say a foolish thing, a fool can say something wise once in awhile.

IN BUSINESS, AS IN LIFE, THE WILL TO SUCCEED CAN OVERCOME ANYTHING

In 1982, a 16-year-old Canadian, Silken Laumann, took up rowing for the first time. Two years later she earned a Bronze Medal for Canada in the Los Angeles Olympics. By the end of 1991, she was the World Champion and World Record Holder in the Single Scull.

Just ten weeks prior to the 1992 Olympics, two German scullers accidentally rammed their bow into Silken's right leg severing five muscle groups and shattering her tibia as well as her dream to win the Women's Single Scull.

Secretly, Silken began weight lifting in her hospital bed. After five operations she began to row again. Unbelievably, just two months after her accident, she competed in Barcelona. Halfway through the race she was in fourth place and in tremendous agony. She reached inside and, telling herself she could overcome the pain, she inched forward, refusing to let up. She took third place, winning a Bronze Medal which, under the circumstances, was nothing short of miraculous.

In 1995, she won the Single's event at the Pan American Games and took a Silver Medal in the 1996 Olympics in Atlanta.

All of us in business should look at this young lady's accomplishments as our motivation to succeed no matter how difficult the situation might seem to be. She is living proof that the human spirit can overcome anything if the will is strong enough.

508
Many people don't look dumb
until they start talking.

509
Wait at least one hour before speaking to someone who has just screwed up.

510
Having it all doesn't necessarily mean
having it all at once.

511
"Strive for businesses that complement each other – like the man who was a veterinarian and a taxidermist: Either way, you get your dog back."
– Mike Buckman

Given a choice between building your business on a large debt or facing a firing squad – choose the firing squad. There's a chance that the firing squad might miss.

513

You Never Go Wrong
Doing The Right Thing

It was 5:45 p.m. on a chilly November evening when I left a meeting at the Grand Hyatt Hotel in New York City. My next appointment was a dinner at Le Cirque with the chairman of a major investment banking firm.

As I walked out of the hotel it began to rain heavily. There wasn't a taxi in sight and Le Cirque was 23 blocks uptown. My Type "A" personality dictated that I couldn't stand with 50 other people waiting for a cab. I started to walk … very fast. As I walked, I kept glancing over my shoulder in the hope that God would send me a taxi.

The midtown traffic was awful. I was actually walking faster than the cars were moving. As I approached 49th Street a taxi pulled in next to me and a lady (obviously sent from heaven) jumped out. About 10 people raced through the rain to grab my cab but I was into the seat in a nanosecond.

As we started up Park Avenue, the driver remarked that he had seen me way back at the Grand Hyatt Hotel. "You looked hassled – like you were very late for something important," he said as we stopped at the light at 53rd Street. "You looked as hassled as that guy over there."

I looked out the window and saw a man walking as fast as I had been. Tired, wet, and cold he was looking over his shoulder. He was obviously late and also asking God to send him a taxi.

I don't know why, because I'd never done such a thing before, but as we drove up next to this man, I rolled down my window and said, "You look like you're in a hurry. Would you like a ride uptown?" In an instant he was in the cab, clearly relieved to be out of the downpour.

We introduced ourselves, but I didn't focus on his name. He mentioned that he worked at the Colgate Company. Since I had several friends working there at the time, I mentioned their names. He said that he knew them. "Great," I said. "What part of the company do you work in?"

"I'm the chairman," he said. Thirty days later, Ruben Mark joined the board of my non-profit organization that provided funding for high-risk, inner-city children.

Since that day, I have always gone out of my way to help other people. It makes you feel good, and you never know who you'll meet.

514

If the water is real murky,
only a fool would dive right in.

515

Mediocre people tend to hire mediocre people.

516

If you see something interesting in a magazine or newspaper, tear it out and circulate it to your colleagues and staff.

517

Even if your entire board of directors votes for a stupid idea, it's still a stupid idea.

518

When considering a new job, review what you've got to do for eight hours and ask yourself how you'd feel if you had to do it for a lifetime.

519

There's never a right way to do a wrong thing.

520

"The best executive is the one who has sense enough to pick good men to do what he wants done, and self-restraint enough to keep from meddling with them while they do it."
– Theodore Roosevelt

521

Striving for excellence is motivating;
striving for perfection is demoralizing.

522

Retirement is that period in life when
"time is no longer money."

523

If you spend too much time at work and put your marriage on the back burner, it is only a matter of time before your marriage will boil over.

"I'm so sorry to hear of your loss, Mrs. Wilson.
But, your husband's group insurance policy
is only valid if he dies in a group."

You Can Always Come Back Tomorrow

Many businesspeople make the mistake of thinking that just because they have flown into a prospect's home city and are now negotiating at his conference table that they must make the deal "right now." Most of the time this isn't true. If the deal isn't fair, consider a polite "thank you anyway," get on the plane, and go home. If they don't call you the next day with improved terms, you can always call them and accept the deal that's on the table.

Many years ago I was traveling in Hong Kong with my wife, who desperately wanted to purchase antique temple carvings. We were staying at the Peninsula Hotel, and the concierge introduced us to an old gentleman named Charlie Wu who knew where to buy absolutely everything.

Charlie took us to a part of Hong Kong that I'm sure very few Westerners ever visited. We parked in an old residential area and walked down a long narrow alley with locals quietly observing us from windows and doorways. It was like being in a *film noir* ... I fully expected Humphrey Bogart to step out of a doorway and light up a Camel at any moment.

We finally stopped at the end of the alley and met Har Kee, who was about 70 years old and did not strike me as the type to be peddling antique temple carvings to Connecticut yuppies.

Har Kee, who spoke very little English, motioned us into a building that should have been torn down 50 years earlier. As we started up five flights of steps with very dim lighting, I became aware that people were watching us on each landing. The smell of that decrepit hallway is still in my memory. About halfway to the fifth floor, my wife decided she no longer needed antique temple carvings and requested that we "Get out of here ... now!" But we kept going.

When we finally reached the top floor, Har Kee unlocked three huge padlocks on a solid steel door that must have weighed 1,000 pounds. The door took all of his strength to open. He motioned us into a dark hallway lit only with a low watt bulb hanging in the middle of the hall on a wire.

There were four large rooms off the hallway, each filled with hundreds of antique temple carvings. To this day we have never seen anything like it. One was more beautiful than the next. My wife was thrilled and moved from room to room collecting carvings.

After about a half-hour, she had chosen five magnificent items. I brought them to Har Kee, who smiled broadly showing his gold tooth ... he looked like someone right out of Central Casting. With no lack of self-confidence, he instantly quoted me $11,500. At first I thought he was quoting me in local currency, but I quickly realized it was U.S. dollars. I may have been unsure about the currency, but the art of negotiation is the same in any culture. I told Mr. Kee I would only spend $3,000 in total. I fully expected that he would counter offer $5-$6,000. He said that the best he could do was $10,800. My wife leaned over and quietly said, "Great ... pay him." With my most serious "this is my final offer" expression, I told Mr. Kee that I could only spend $4,000 ... "Take it or leave it." The smile immediately went away. Mr. Kee fired off some strong Chinese, turned off the light in the room, and started out the door. My wife couldn't believe that I wasn't going to buy the carvings. I told her not to say another word and we walked towards the steel door. I expected Mr. Kee to stop at the door and offer a counter proposal, but he didn't. He closed the door, snapped all three padlocks, and started down the stairs. I waited for him to re-negotiate when we got down to the street. Wrong. He simply bowed and said goodbye to our guide Charlie.

We started back up the long alley. My wife was furious with me. I told her that this guy had thousands of antique carvings and wouldn't let us get away. I also knew that we could always have

Charlie call him tomorrow to tell him that we had changed our minds. As we neared the end of the alley, I wanted to look back to see if Mr. Kee was behind us, but I didn't dare. We reached the end of the alley and turned the corner. At that instant Mr. Kee, appearing as if by magic from behind us, grabbed my shoulder and said, "OK ... $5,000." I immediately countered with $4,500. Mr. Kee smiled, gold tooth shining in the sun, and said, "OK."

We then walked all the way back down the alley, up five flights of stairs, unlocked the padlocks, and opened the huge steel door ... but it was worth it. Knowing I could always come back tomorrow had saved me $7,000.

526
Luck is what happens
when preparation meets opportunity.

527
"Life is funny; if you refuse to accept nothing but the best, you very often get it."
– Somerset Maugham

"What do you mean you stopped answering
the phone because it's always for me?!"

529
Always be working on your next promotion.

530
Anyone in business who burns his bridges
better be a damn good swimmer.

531
Even the greatest skaters
sometimes fall through the ice.

532
If you want advice, try to ask the person who "wrote
the book" not the person who "read the book."

533
If you are in charge and you stop rowing, don't be
surprised if the rest of your crew stops, too.

534
Executives who resist change because they think
they are on the right track should remember that
they can get run over if they just stand on that track
too long.

535

Never mistake a slogan for a solution.

536

Act successful if you want to be successful.

537

Your example is more important than your advice.

538

People who say winning isn't everything,
never win.

539

People who make business decisions with their hearts usually end up with heartburn.

540

The first thing that happens when you become chairperson is that all your acquaintances from high school, who you haven't heard from in thirty years, remember that they were your best friend.

When a consultant tells you that his fee is "only" $50,000 upfront, offer $60,000 but stipulate you'll pay when the job is finished.

A close friend in the consulting business once told me that the justification of fees was one of the most difficult aspects of his job. The more senior the consultant, the greater his or her contacts and the easier it is to get the job done. But if the job looks too easy, the client resents paying a large fee. When confronted with resistance, my friend always tells his clients the following tale:

In 1970, NASA had four astronauts circling the moon. Suddenly, the entire communications center went down and Houston Control could not communicate with the astronauts. NASA technicians couldn't locate the problem, and the mission director was in near panic. In desperation, he called in a well-known communications consultant to help.

This small, slightly-built consultant arrived complete with tiny bow tie, horn-rimmed glasses, and a small electronic tool kit belted around his waist. He circled the control center slowly three times, studying the computers and relays. Finally, he stopped in front of a small relay, reached into his pocket and took out a small rubber mallet.

He carefully tapped one particular relay and the entire communications center came back on line instantly. The director was elated.

A week later the director received a bill for $50,000 from the consultant. Irate, the director called the consultant and demanded an explanation for such a charge for tapping a relay with a rubber mallet. The consultant said, "Oh you've misunderstood my bill. I charged you $1,000 for tapping the relay and $49,000 for knowing where to tap."

542
It is easier to get forgiveness than permission.

543
If you are staff, spend some time on the line.
If you are on the line, spend some time with the staff.

544
The proper use of personal notepaper can sometimes be more important than the use of corporate stationery.

ALWAYS MAINTAIN
A POSITIVE ATTITUDE

Many years ago, a large American shoe manufacturer sent two sales reps out to different parts of the Australian Outback to see if they could drum up some business among the Aborigines. Some days later, the company received messages from both agents. The first one said: "No business here – the natives don't wear shoes." The second one said: "Great opportunity here – the natives don't wear shoes!"

546

When you need financing, "no" is not an acceptable answer. It's just your cue to look elsewhere.

547

Know where to get your industry's news and gossip.

548

Your advertising has to be at least as good as your product … but more importantly, your product must be as good as your advertising.

549

Some of the most important people in your company are in the mailroom … they know everyone and everything. Spend time visiting them – they might just enlighten you.

550

When you meet a businessperson who tells you it isn't the money but the principle, you've met either a fool or a liar.

551

"You miss 100 percent of the shots you never take ..."
– Wayne Gretzky

552

People who "play office"
should go back to kindergarten.

553

Any meaningful idea in business should be able to
be stated in less than one minute.

554

The problem with successful small companies is
that as soon as they get big, they usually forget what
made them successful.

555

"When you reach for the stars, you may not quite
get one, but you won't come up with a handful of
mud, either."

– Leo Burnett
Chairman
Leo Burnett Co., Inc.

556

To build a winning business team,
hire people who can replace you.

557

When you've made your point, shut up and sit
down. When you've tried and failed to make your
point, shut up and sit down.

558

When you've got a good banker, take him to lunch
from time to time ... not just when you need money.

559

The executive on the fast track doesn't wait for
tomorrow. He does it now.

560

"Work done with little effort
is likely to yield little results."
– B.C. Forbes

561
Always Carry A Yellow Pad

The yellow pad is not only a tool for gathering information, it is the ultimate corporate fashion accessory and much more. The uses of the pad are legion, but some of the top reasons to carry one are:

1. No matter where you are going or what you are doing, people will believe it is business-related.

2. It allows you the right to pass any receptionist without being challenged.

3. It allows you the right to leave the building and go home without issue.

4. It allows you the right to return from lunch late.

5. It looks more professional than showing up at a meeting without one.

6. It gives the impression that you are more in control.

7. It provides the ability to escape from boring meetings by writing to your mother.

8. It allows you the ability to actually take notes. Besides creating the impression that you are paying attention, the yellow pad helps you actually to do so. Careful notes reduce the ambiguities inherent in receiving instructions.

Ben Frankly says ...

"In business, as in life, ever notice how
the empty can makes the loudest noise?"

563

Praise loudly and criticize quietly.

564

"I would rather lose in a cause that will someday win, than win in a cause that will someday lose."
– Woodrow Wilson

565

Never treat your subordinates as inferiors.

566

Your memory is made of paper ... keep great notes.

567

Unless you enjoy playing Russian roulette with five bullets, never cheat on your expense account.

568

Given a sufficient number of people and an adequate amount of time, one can create insurmountable opposition to most inconsequential ideas.

THERE ARE USUALLY MULTIPLE SOLUTIONS
TO ALL PROBLEMS

Years ago, my wife wanted to have the four-foot deep basement of our New York City brownstone (originally built in 1823) dug out to a full eight feet to accommodate a laundry and a gym.

What a challenge! There was no way to get construction equipment into the basement so I hired manual laborers to remove the dirt with five-gallon buckets on a rope through the original coal chute in front of the building.

On the fifth day, my lead digger approached me with a problem – they had dug around a huge rock in the middle of the floor. It was about six feet in diameter and was one of those very smooth stones that you could not even chip with a sledgehammer.

I called in an engineer who believed that we could drill into the center with a carbon drill, place a very small amount of dynamite inside, and crack the rock into small enough pieces to carry it up the coal chute. Cost: $2,800, which was a lot of money in those days. Another contractor wanted to bring in a pneumatic air hammer. His charges were estimated at $2,200. The rock had to go, but what was the right way to get rid of it? Suddenly, I had a thought.

I asked my lead digger how long it would take to dig a hole 6 feet-by-6 feet right next to the rock. He said, "About three hours." At $10 per hour, I gave him the go-ahead.

When the hole was completed, we pushed the rock into the hole. It completely vanished at a total cost of $30. The basement turned out beautifully and functioned as planned.

570
Corporate bullies create corporate turnover.

571
If they don't call you back in a week,
they probably won't.

572
If you require at least eight hours sleep a night, it is important that you have a great relationship with your spouse ... and never tell her you own more than $50 million in life insurance.

573

"When you win, nothing hurts."
– Joe Namath

574

"If you can touch it, you can catch it."
– Vince Lombardi
Former NFL Coach

575

"Buy on the rumor. Sell on the news."
– Bernard Baruch

576

"If you shoot, shoot to kill."
– J. Edgar Hoover

577

When you make a mistake, admit it.

578

When you find you don't love your job,
look for another.

The low bidder is usually someone
who is left wondering what he left out.

580
IF YOU WANT TO SUCCEED, FOCUS ON WHY IT WILL WORK ... NOT ON WHY IT WON'T

In business, as in life, every issue, decision or opportunity contains both a positive and negative aspect. All too often in the corporate world, many executives focus on why something won't work rather than on the ways in which something will work. After hours of discussion, negatively focused executives will have arrived at the best reason *not* to do something. These types tend to be known as the Abominable No-Men. Had they spent the same time focused on how to make something happen, they may well have created a new product or service that would provide greater revenue to their company.

A few years ago, I funded the seed capital for a start-up company called Greenfield Healthy Foods that made wholesome, great tasting snacks. Once I saw how much consumers loved these snacks, I set out to raise several million dollars in additional capital. The economy was awful at that time and it was probably the worst time to try to raise money since the Great Depression. But I was positive that the company's concept was correct. I wanted to sell 30 percent of the company. Over 100 investors turned me down because they focused on why the company *wouldn't* work – but 16 high net worth individuals focused on why it *would* work and I raised all of the capital required. By the company's third year, its sales were going straight up and we ultimately sold the company to the Campbell Soup Company for a great return. When we exited the company, our products were in 67,000 stores with sales of $52 million.

Clearly, Greenfield would never have been started much less have become successful had everyone involved not had very positive attitudes. In these difficult economic times, it is essential for all chief executives to maintain positive attitudes if they want their companies to grow. A negative perspective limits self-confidence and the ability to take necessary risks. If you focus hard enough on why something won't work, chances are it won't.

581
Shoot high.

582
Don't take calls when in meetings.

583
Revise your five-year plan every six months.

584
You can't steal second base
if you always keep one foot on first.

585
If the only tool in your toolbox is a hammer
you tend to treat all opportunities as nails.

586
Never condone racism or sexism
or bigotry of any kind.

587
Never knock the competition. Find out what they
are doing right and tell your employees.

588
WHEN YOU THINK THINGS CAN'T GET WORSE, THERE'S ALWAYS TOMORROW
John Mariucci, when coaching the U.S. Olympic
Hockey team, became impatient with his young
and inexperienced team. During one particularly
low moment he screamed: "Every day you guys
look worse and worse ... today you played like
tomorrow!"

589
Those who fail to prepare
are always prepared to fail.

590
Leave your business at your office or you'll leave
your marriage at your lawyer's.

591
"There's a fine line between being colorful and a
real asshole, and I hope I'm still just colorful."
– Ted Turner

592
MODESTY IS FAR MORE IMPRESSIVE
At a luncheon with photographer Yousuf Karsh and
his wife, the astronaut Neil Armstrong, who became
the first human to set foot on the moon, politely
asked the couple about the many places they had
visited. Mr. Karsh responded: "Mr. Armstrong,
you've walked on the moon. We would much
rather hear about your travels." "But that's the only
place I've ever been," remarked Armstrong,
apologetically.

Sometimes in business, as in life,
the dragon wins!
Get over it.

594

A career shouldn't be a quest for perfection,
but for a high batting average.

595

Executive personalities can sometimes be measured
by their actions. For example, in driving, there are
two types of executive motorists – those who drive
as if they owned the road, and those who drive as if
they owned the car.

596

Don't envy executives who have everything …
most of them haven't paid for it yet.

597

Management recruiters like to offer good jobs to
people who already have good jobs.

598

Tell an employee something about someone else
only if you don't mind someone else finding out.

599

"Advice is what we ask for when we already know the answer but wish we didn't."

– Erica Jong

600

Most of one's unhappiness is the direct result of comparing yourself to others.

601

Most executives who must control
are actually terrified of losing control.

602

People who don't work with great enthusiasm are a danger to the entire business and should be fired with great enthusiasm.

603

"One machine can do the work of 100 ordinary men. No machine can do the work of one extraordinary man."

– Henry Ford

604

Act and look professional
and people will think you are.

605

Reacting is much easier than thinking and failing is
much easier than success.

606

Try to remember all names and faces,
not just the "important" ones.

607

The greatest mistake an executive can make is to be
afraid of making a mistake.

608

In business, as in life, size up your competition.
Consider Dave Marr, the famous PGA Golf
Champion's quote: "Never bet with anyone you
meet on the first tee who has a deep suntan and a
1-iron in his bag."

609

Watch your manners. Others are.

610

Knowledge becomes wisdom only after it has been put to good use.

611

Have an office party every year.

612

Reward employees who have good ideas …
it's contagious.

613

"Market research has established beyond the shadow of a doubt that the egg is a sad and sorry product and that it obviously will not sell. Because, after all, eggs won't stand up by themselves, they roll too easily, are too easily broken, require special packaging, look alike, are difficult to open, won't stack on the shelf."

– Robert Pliskin
Former Vice President
Benton & Bowles

Ben Frankly says ...

"Business is like riding a bicycle.
Either you keep up your speed or
you'll fall down."

615
Learn to recognize
when people are not listening to you.

616
The more you need your job,
the worse you will be treated.

617
Anyone who thinks he or she is indispensable
should stick a finger in a bowl of water and notice
how long the hole stays there after the finger is
pulled out.

618
To improve your odds of success,
be the first one in and the last one out.

619
Brilliant ideas are those that were first thought to be
wrong but later shown to be obvious.

620

If you covet your boss' job,
learn how to do it better than he or she does.

621

Establish a goal that someday you'll take the corner
office. When it happens, modify your goal to get
the corner office on a higher floor.

622

Know your receptionist by name,
or she might forget yours.

623

Join a club that at least one member of your board
belongs to.

624

"If you don't do it excellently, don't do it at all.
Because if it's not excellent, it won't be profitable
or fun, and if you're not in business for fun or
profit, what the hell are you doing there?"

– Robert Townsend
Author of *Up The Organization*
and Former CEO of Avis

625
Do it right the first time.

626
If your company offers educational opportunities, make use of them.

627
Jerks lose their tempers.

628
Send handwritten thank you notes to every customer at least once a year.

629
Don't blame others for your errors.
If you're responsible, take the hit.

630
Never insult the waiter until *after* he or she has brought your food.

631
Walk around the office at least once a day.

632
Some executives dream of success while others stay awake and achieve it.

633
Get at least three bids for every job.

634
Buy stuff from the lobby newsstand or someday it might not be there.

635
Capital is the fuel of business. How far do you think your car would run on credit?

636
"Incompetence knows no barriers of time or place."
– Laurence J. Peter
Author of *The Peter Principle*

Original Instant Messaging

638

Write memos to yourself on subjects and file them carefully.

639

Don't negotiate against yourself. Wait for someone to tell you what they think it's worth first.

640

If you think something is wrong, it probably is. Always respect your instincts.

641

In the race for success, the speed of the leader determines the pace of the pack.

642

It has been said that it's awful hard to climb the ladder of life with a bag of gold on your shoulder … but it's just as hard with a bag of dirt.

NEVER LET PERSONAL SETBACKS
DISTRACT YOU FROM YOUR BUSINESS

In 1981, I hired a painter to re-paint the front of our brownstone. One morning I rode up on the scaffold with him to look at the work. When we reached the fourth floor the scaffold broke. I dropped four stories and landed on an iron fence below. A post went right into my chest, and I broke my nose and other bones in my face. I was rushed to Bellevue Hospital in critical condition.

The doctors told my wife that since I was in great shape, I had a good chance of survival. I had been training for my third New York City Marathon. Every day for months I had run fifteen miles and was probably in the best condition anyone falling four stories would want to be in.

Although there is never a good time for this sort of thing, it could not have happened at a worse time for my business. I was in the final days of launching a trade show at the New York Coliseum. I had a fortune invested in this business and each day that I was not selling booth space in the show put the entire venture at risk.

It was this motivation that forced me to get out of the hospital bed two days after the fall, so I could make phone calls to prospects from the pay phone in the hallway at Bellevue. My doctors and my wife went crazy, but over their objections, I continued to work.

On the fourth day after the fall, the doctors told my wife to take me home. They felt that I was better off working at home than from a cart that I had set up in the hallway at their hospital.

Less than a week after falling from the roof of my building, I returned to the office. My staff could not look at me, but the show sold out and I saved my business.

644
Misfortunes usually come in by the door left open for them.

645
Never have more than two drinks on an airplane unless it's the return flight.

646
If you get to the boardroom through the bedroom, the honeymoon is usually very short.

647

Some executives succeed because they are destined to ... but most executives succeed because they are determined to.

648

A good driver knows when to put the pedal to the metal and when to hit the brakes.

649

Mediocre executives are frightened by new ideas. Successful ones are frightened by old ideas.

650

Take your assistant to lunch ... but not too often.

651

Ann Landers said: "Don't accept that your dog wags his tail when he sees you as conclusive evidence that you are wonderful." The same holds true in business. Self-evaluation is very important.

Some days you are the pigeon –
some days you are the statue.

653

The smallest action is always better
than the grandest intention.

654

You can put your faith in the rabbit's foot if you
want, but remember ... it didn't work too well for
the rabbit.

655

Some people climb the corporate ladder and achieve
great success ... others simply become great
climbers.

656

To get where you want to go, you sometimes have
to go in the opposite direction.

657

Beat your boss at golf and he'll want to play more
often. If he doesn't, you're as good as fired and it
doesn't matter.

658

The only thing better than a great dream
is a financed great dream.

659

"You can't score
if you keep the bat on your shoulder."
– Casey Stengel

660

Don't shoot the messenger.
Give him a strong letter to take back.

661

In business you cannot discover new oceans
unless you have the courage to leave the shore.

662

Demand excellence from every employee …
including yourself.

663

"Keep your face to the sunshine
and you cannot see a shadow."
– Helen Keller

664

Come to work at 6:00 a.m.
and leave at 8:00 p.m. once a month.

665

Remember all who are working at 6:00 a.m.
and 8:00 p.m. and give them a raise.

666

If no one is ever at work at 6:00 a.m. or 8:00 p.m.,
your company is in trouble.

667

Send your customers "something" in the mail often
… it really doesn't matter what it is. You just want
them to know that you're still out there when it's
time for them to buy another one of what you sell.

668

Never pay for work before it's completed.

669

The best consultants find out the facts by interviewing your employees. Why can't you do that?

670

"It takes five years of very hard work
to become an instant success."
– William A. Shea, Jr.
Shea & Gould

671

Fire all regional sales managers whose best customers don't know them by their first name.

672

Theodore Geisel (also known as "Dr. Suess") had his first book turned down by 28 publishers before it finally became one of the world's best-selling stories.

Many times, determination and perseverance are the keys to success.

673

"The good news is that I think the economy is getter better. The bad news is that your 401(k) is now a 201(k)."

KEEP CURRENT –
READ A NEWSPAPER EVERY DAY.

One morning I read in *The New York Times* Business Section that a subsidiary of a major corporation had posted a loss that could only be described as fatal. I thought, "If I were the chief financial officer of the parent corporation, I would like to sell this division in the worst way." I picked up the phone and made a cold call to the CFO. I got his assistant on the phone and told her I had a client interested in buying the ailing division. It took only seconds for the CFO to be on the line inviting me to stop by and see him at the earliest opportunity. I went over that afternoon and met the CFO. Sure enough he was more than ready to sell the division. When he asked me who my client was, I told him that I wasn't in a position to divulge that information at that time.

I left his office with all the necessary financials and went directly to my office. I made a list of every company in the same business category that might be in the market to expand. I started cold-calling the president of each company. I told each assistant that I was calling to see if the president might be interested in the purchase of a competing company. Every president took my call. On the eighth call, I found a company in the expansion mode. Sixty days later the deal was done and I earned a large

six-figure finder's fee. To me this was living proof
that you can get your job through *The New York Times*.

675
Build strong alliances.

676
Drink and corporate drive don't mix.

677
Resist giving your bosses advice. Offer suggestions
that allow them to reach the same conclusion.

678
To make a strong first impression,
have a firm handshake.

679
SOME PEOPLE ARE LUCKY AND SOME ARE NOT
John Paul Getty, the oil executive and billionaire,
once received a request from a magazine for a short
article that explained his great success. The
billionaire obligingly wrote: "Some people find oil
– others don't."

680

Treat your employees as you treat your boss.

681

Build a good business card file.
Contacts make all the difference.

682

TRUST YOUR INSTINCTS

Not long ago at a One To One Dinner, Bill Russell,
who I think is one of the greatest basketball players
to have ever played the game, and an amazing
person, told me the following story and his moral is
one that I live by every day:

> When I was in the 11th grade, I was cut from
> the junior varsity basketball team. Our varsity
> coach then approached me and asked me to
> play on the varsity team. "I just got cut from
> the JV Team," I said. His answer: "I'm not
> coaching the JV."

The moral of this story is to go with your instincts
and you just might be right.

683

"Never underestimate a man
who overestimates himself."
– Franklin D. Roosevelt

684

If you are going to buy a dead horse, make sure you
either know CPR or where to sell the parts.

685

Whatever you are … try to be a great one.

686

Sometimes the most impressive or intelligent thing
you can say in a meeting is nothing.

687

"Only the fittest will survive, and the fittest will be
the ones who understand their office's politics."
– Jean Hollands

Ben Frankly says ...

"A fat lawsuit is never as smart
as a lean compromise."

689

NEGOTIATE FROM STRENGTH

Many years ago, I was a principal in a transaction with a well-known financier. Fortunately, this man was on my side ... a major investment banking firm was on the other. The final negotiating session was held in the financier's office around a huge circular conference table made of plate glass.

Twelve executives sat around the glass table, which was strewn with papers and stacks of files. Also on the table was a magnificent Steuben glass ashtray weighing at least fifteen pounds.

We were heatedly arguing a final point that was worth about $100,000 in this multimillion dollar deal. At a crucial moment, my partner stood up, blasted the room with a stream of shouted profanities, picked up the ashtray and slammed it down into the center of the glass table. The table ceased to exist and shattered glass carpeted the room.

It is hard to express how shocking it was for twelve grown men to be suddenly sitting in a circle no longer occupied by a table.

The other side, white with shock, collapsed, conceded the $100,000-deal point, and promptly left the meeting.

As soon as they were out of the room, I asked my partner if he had gone completely insane. He looked at me calmly and said, "That table cost me $10,000. I go through about twelve of them a year. At an average profit of $90,000 per table, I'm more than a million dollars ahead in tables each year."

690
Many times genius is disguised
as intelligent persistence.

691
Try not to waste time selling something to someone who isn't the decision-maker.

692
Rule #1: The customer is always right.
Rule #2: If the customer is ever wrong, re-read Rule #1.

693
Awards, recognition, and exposure don't pay the bills. The true test of any marketing effort is in the amount of revenue produced.

694
Share the credit.

695
Before borrowing money from a friend,
decide which you need most.

696
Never hire a security guard who weighs less than
150 lbs. or more than 250 lbs.

697
Any decent executive can identify a wrong answer –
it takes real skill to identify a wrong question.

698
Don't delegate office security or fire safety,
and never take either for granted.

699
If the meeting is very important, don't fly overseas
on a night flight. Take an extra day, go on a day
flight, and get a good night's sleep.

700
Fall behind on deadlines
and you'll fall behind in business.

701
If you are successful in business, don't show up at your kid's school with your driver and your limo.

702
Reconfirm all business meetings – especially if you have to fly to get there.

703
Anytime you must "rush" to make a good business deal, pass. Another good deal will always come along.

704
Employees are like children. Don't expect them to listen to your advice and to ignore your example.

If you pay peanuts, you get monkeys.

706

Successful executives do not spend valuable time finding faults, they spend time finding remedies.

707

Experienced business travelers know that motel mattresses are better on the side away from the phone.

708

Executives who speak with more claret than clarity usually end up speaking to themselves.

709

There is no limit to what you can achieve if you don't mind who gets the credit.

710

To improve in business, listen carefully to all your enemies ... they are the ones that will bluntly point out your faults.

711

Brainpower in business
is more powerful than horsepower.

712

SOMETIMES COMPLEX PROBLEMS CAN BE SOLVED WITH SIMPLE SOLUTIONS

For many years I served on the board of a K-12 independent private school. One of our most successful programs was designed to assist new students in getting acclimated to their new environment. Obviously, when a child joins a new school it can be a very intimidating experience. The child is an outsider, full of anxieties, with no circle of friends – they don't even have someone to sit with at lunchtime. We created an extremely simple solution to reduce this social anxiety. We assigned the family of one of the more "outgoing" students to act as a "family mentor" to the new student and his or her parents. Ideally, these families would get together socially one month prior to the beginning of the new school year and discuss the student's social issues and the parents' administrative concerns. When school started, our new students hit the ground running. They were no longer alone, but connected to a circle of friends organized by our mentoring student.

713

Never ignore the infrastructure …
it's what holds everything together.

714

"When considering an investment, remember that
the future is longer than the present."
– William A. Shea, Jr.

715

Don't sell the American public short …
they will pay a bit extra for quality.

716

Remember, it's really hard to make a comeback
when you haven't been anywhere.

717

When you step in the gutter,
you always get mud on your shoes.

Stay away from low-life people and low-life
situations.

718

The harder you work,
the luckier you get.

719

Strive to be consistent.

720

Make sure someone in the company
owns a pickup truck.

721

Nothing for nothing is nothing.

If you don't put any real effort into something, you
can't expect to realize any measurable gains.

722

The road to success is always under construction.

723

Make a photocopy of the contents of your wallet
before you lose it.

Never eat chili before a board meeting.

725

Never contradict your boss at a board meeting.

726

The large print giveth
and the small print taketh away.

727

Fix it now, or it will still be there tomorrow –
only worse.

728

"You can't solve a problem
in the mind-set that created it."
– Albert Einstein

729

Worry about little expenses.   Remember a small
leak will ultimately sink any great ship.

730

Never talk business with your colleagues in
elevators, the restroom, or when you're alone in the
customer's meeting room.

731
Get Paid What You Are Really Worth

As your time at a corporation stretches from months to years, an interesting thing happens: Management gets to know all your good qualities and also your bad qualities. When a possible promotion for you comes along, management evaluates the "total you" for the position. This includes identifying your faults.

If a higher position becomes available at another company and you become a candidate, the management of the new company really doesn't know the "total you." They know only what you tell them and what's written on your résumé. Even if they check your references, your references will only highlight your more golden qualities. Because of this, you will always look better and be more promotable to another company.

If you receive a promotion within your present company, you can look for a 10-20% increase in compensation along with your new title and responsibilities. If you change companies for a better position, you can earn at least 30 percent more because people pay more to motivate you into leaving a place where you are safe and comfortable. If you have to relocate to a different town, your compensation will be even higher.

In your interview with another company, you should tell them the pay you need to come over to them. Start at a minimum of 40 percent more than you are paid at your present company. You can always trade dollars for "perks" if you are too high: "Okay, I'll take less cash – but I'll need a company car."

Sometimes an interviewer might ask you what your current salary is. It's really none of their business, but if they are nosy enough to ask, you should be smart enough to tell them a salary number that reflects your true value to your corporation, not just your take-home pay.

732
"There's a better way to do it. Find it."
– Thomas Edison

733
"Executives who take control make their company happen. The other ones get bogged down in a sea of bureaucracy."

– J.E. Antonini
Former Chairman and CEO
Kmart Corporation

734
Sue first.

735
Always remember: a secret is something you tell to one person at a time.

736
"I may be a slow walker,
but I never walk backward."
– Abraham Lincoln

737
Support your suppliers … buy their products.

738
No matter what the situation, always act as you think the chairman would act.

739
To increase the odds of speaking directly to a top executive, call his or her office before 8:30 a.m. or after 5:30 p.m. Chances are he or she will pick up the phone.

Ben Frankly says ...

"The carrot is one hundred times more effective than the stick – and you don't have to worry about being hit back!"

WHAT "GETTING IT DONE" IS ALL ABOUT

Although many of us in business control our "kingdoms" from behind a desk each day and do not have the opportunity for heroic efforts worthy of a movie script, the following story from my book, *A Spirit of Greatness; Stories from the Employees of American Airlines,* is inspirational nonetheless. In this extraordinary story about employee dedication, First Officer Robert Dunning praised the dedication of his co-worker, American Airlines pilot Captain Stuart Kingman:

El Niño hit hard wreaking havoc on land and sea and greatly impacting air travel. Captain Stuart Kingman was on call and asked to report to work immediately. As he started down the road to the airport from his mountain ridge home he soon discovered that a mudslide had completely closed the road.

Committed to making his flight, Captain Kingman called his brother-in-law to meet him on the other side of the mountain, changed into hiking clothes, and with his uniform in his backpack, made his way on foot over the mudslide to his brother-in-law, arriving at the airport in time for his trip.

While most of us will never know a morning commute so dramatic, it speaks volumes about character and commitment to a job when an employee is willing to go to such extraordinary lengths to show up for work.

742
If you want to communicate effectively,
be careful that you don't say too much.

743
A promotion always goes to the employee who is slightly better than the rest of the candidates.

744
Ride the truck with your delivery people at least once a year.

745
Anyone rude enough to ask your compensation
should be given a much higher number.

746
One of the biggest mistakes you can make in business is to *not* compliment your employees – often.

747

Temper gets you in trouble.
Pride keeps you there.

748

Show up unannounced at a field office at least twice a year.

749

"Tell me, I forget; show me, I remember;
involve me, I understand."
– Ernst Wynder, M.D.
Former President
American Health Foundation

750

Always sit at the head of the table
when attending meetings.

751

Upon making it to the summit, your first move should be to turn around and offer a hand up to the person behind you.

752

Keep a spare toilet kit in your office.

753

Don't be negative. No one likes a rain cloud.
People gravitate to the sunshine.

754

If it sounds too good to be true, it usually is.

755

Teach key employees everything they need to know
about your job.

756

When your ideas meet with silence, don't assume
consent. People just may not be listening.

757

Call your switchboard at least once a month and ask
for yourself. It may shock you to find out how
difficult it is to reach you.

On Wall Street it is widely believed that religion was invented to keep the poor from killing the rich.

759

Happiness is a positive cash flow.

760

Salvage something from all mistakes …
learn from them.

761

Know when to cut your losses and move on.

762

"Lord, grant that I may always desire
more than I can accomplish."
– Michelangelo

763

In business, as in sailing, it is easier to adjust the
sails than to try to direct the wind.

764

Be extra careful when doing business with someone
who has nothing to lose.

765

It's better to act than to react.

766

Think big, act big ... and big things happen.

767

Don't ever be afraid to employ people who are smarter than you.

768

Don't mistake control for leadership.

769

If you really want to know what's going on in your business, read your customer mail once a month.

770

Giving a poor man a fish might make you feel good. But try to imagine how great you'll feel if you give him a fishing pole and take the time to teach him how to fish.

771
"Corporations pay for performance,
not for potential."
– Robert Downey
Goldman Sachs

772
Try not to bring a lawyer to a business meeting.

773
Attacks must be answered.
An assertion unanswered is an assertion agreed to.

774
Successful people know never to give up …
but to follow up.

775
Nothing happens until someone sells something.

776
If you have to give business cards to your good
customers, you haven't seen them enough.

777
Throw out the biggest and lowest bids.

778
No matter how hard you try
you can't put a good edge on bad steel.

779
Never admit to anyone that you have re-gripped
your golf ball retriever.

780
Keep to both the letter and the spirit of your
agreements.

781
Always take a call from a headhunter … you never
know when you'll need him.

782
Any customer dumb enough to ask your profit
margin should be given a much lower number.

"Why can't my employees be more specific?
Which lake? What kind of kite?"

784

Avoid buying a new piece of equipment for your business unless you know exactly when and how it will pay for itself.

785

Don't be afraid that your computer will start to think like you ... be afraid that you will start to think like your computer.

786

Don't lose customers. Working with a new customer takes 25% more effort than doing the same work with an established customer. It is far less expensive to fix the problem.

787

The successful executive knows that wisdom comes from good judgment, good judgment comes from experience, and experience comes from bad judgment. Employees who make mistakes (and learn from them) are very valuable assets ... more so than employees who don't take any chances at all.

MAKING THE NON-TRADITIONAL METHOD WORK

When we started our food company, Greenfield Healthy Foods, everyone told us that we would never be able to get a new food company off the ground without a large advertising budget and slotting fees paid to supermarket retailers.

Since we didn't have any marketing funds, we decided to approach the grocery industry in a non-traditional way. Our plan was to first build our reputation and some income through health food stores where shelf space is somewhat easier to obtain.

Since we produced cookies and brownies that were fat-free, made with all natural ingredients, and tasted great, we received almost instant success from the health food class of trade. In the case of most healthy foods, the box usually tastes slightly better than the cookies – not so with Greenfield. Once we started, we quickly achieved national sales of over $1 million.

Before we would be ready for our entry into the grocery industry I needed to take one more marketing step – into the airline industry. We were successful in getting our "single serve" packages on five major airlines. Millions of airline passengers were now being introduced to our snacks. We had our address and phone number printed on the package and almost right away we began receiving calls and letters from people across the country asking where they could buy our snacks in their local markets.

We started a campaign to call as many of the people who wrote us as possible. We offered to send them a free case of products if they would take the empty boxes to their local retail grocery store and demand that they carry our products. The campaign was an instant success. It worked so well that I became obsessed with calling customers. We would start calling people in upper New England at 6:00 p.m., and by 11:00 p.m. we would be calling people in California. My family thought I had gone completely crazy but I knew I was breaking new ground in the retail food industry and it was addictive.

When we finally sold our business, our products were in 67,000 stores across the nation and we never paid a penny in slotting fees.

789
If you're not sure whether to do it or not … do it.

790

"It is easier to be nice than nasty ...
and it conserves energy."
– Charlotte Ford

791

For every complaint you receive, assume there are two dozen people who didn't write.

792

If you study the statistics, you'll find that generous people have far fewer emotional problems.

793

When naming a new product, always remember that Americans don't like to buy something they can't pronounce.

794

The history of business teaches us that, as bad as things are now, they will be "the good old days" ten years from now.

Ben Frankly says ...

"If you aren't happy with what you've got now, what makes you think you'll be happier with more?"

796
Always be learning.

797
When you want something done quickly,
give it to the busiest person in your office.

798
Avoid making decisions your employees can make.

799
In business, being scared half to death only works
twice.

800
BE EARLY FOR MEETINGS
My very first boss demanded punctuality at
meetings. He installed a lock on the conference
room door. If the staff meeting was scheduled to
start at 9:00 a.m. sharp, he would lock the door at
precisely 9:00 a.m. and refuse to open it. You only
needed to be locked out once to be motivated never
to be late again. To this day, I try to be early for all
meetings.

801

Never allow yourself to be bullied.

802

The longer the title, the less important the person.

803

On long business trips,
ship your luggage via Federal Express.

804

In business, your most important asset
is your reputation.

805

Innovation is vital in business. It's like the guy who couldn't fix the customer's brakes ... so he made the horn louder.

806

Always negotiate on a deadline: 90% of the agreement will come in the last 10% of the time available.

807
DON'T EVEN THINK ABOUT RESPONDING TO CALL-WAITING – IN FACT, DITCH IT.

Having the newest technology is not always right for business. Call-waiting is the perfect example. Call-waiting is a telephone service that, I am convinced, was expressly designed to annoy as many people as possible in as short a period of time as possible. When you are in the middle of an important call with someone who has call-waiting, there is a little beep when a second call comes in, and then the following usually happens:

1. He or she will probably cut you off while trying to connect with the other party. The silent message here is that you are not important enough for his or her undivided attention.

2. Assuming you are not cut off while waiting, you completely lose your train of thought, to say nothing of the continuity of your presentation.

3. In the midst of the other call, the person you were speaking with forgets what you were saying.

4. You get a knot in your stomach waiting for the other party to come back on the line.

5. The new caller gets a rude fast shuffle so the person you were speaking with can get back to you.

Nobody except the phone company wins from call-waiting. On balance, let it go to voicemail.

808
Support businesses that support education.

809
If you don't drive your business,
you will be driven out of business.

810
Don't ask a tire salesman if you need new tires.

811
Unless job applicants have also coached Little League, worked in a soup kitchen, helped the Salvation Army, or done some other community service, don't hire them.

"You know you've been traveling too much when you come home and dial '9' to get an outside line."

813

"I've never been impressed by someone who does eight hours work in twelve."

– Ralph Giannola
   Former Vice President, Marketing
   Marriott Corporation

814

If you don't use the prospect's first name in your presentation, you aren't a great salesperson.

815

Employees who like their jobs will like their customers.

816

No matter where you're going,
always carry a business card.

817

Decisions should not be made because they are easy, cheap, or because everyone agrees. They should only be made because they are right.

818

You know it's time to retire when nobody knows the difference.

819

TREAT PROBLEMS LIKE NEW OPPORTUNITIES

When I started my career with American Airlines they were not computerized at their flight departure gates, and they used a manual seat-selection system. Obviously, the gate agent would assign window and aisle seats first and the less desirable center seats last. This created a problem with businessmen who arrived late and hated being crowded between two other passengers.

To solve this problem, I would put a circle around the window or aisle seat assigned to any attractive ladies who boarded the plane. When a businessman became irate over a center seat, I would reassign them to a seat next to one of my magnificent female passengers and tell them, "Trust me. This will be a great flight. I've seated you next to someone very nice."

This one simple solution to a vexing problem earned me several dozen letters of commendation from passengers.

820

If you accept free tickets,
don't complain about the show.

821

There is almost nothing in this world that some
dumb executive can't make of poorer quality and
sell for a cheaper price.

822

If you pick up the phone, you own the problem.
Deliver the answer.

823

Some executives tend to complicate everything.
Consider the guy who thinks the best way to feed
the birds is to give more oats to the horses.

824

Accept the fact that half of your advertising dollar
will be wasted and that you will never know which half.

825

Just because you're often right
doesn't mean you're always right.

826

Get what you can and keep what you have
and you will someday be rich.

827

In business, the only disease worse than alcoholism
is egotism.

828

"When the boss lets his hair down too much, he
ends up like Rodney Dangerfield. No respect."
– Lee Iacocca

829

When you need to know if you trust a man, ask
yourself if you would play poker with him over the
telephone.

"…you know that stock we bought so you
could retire at 65? Well, we need to move
your retirement back a bit … to 120!"

831

Worry about the careers of those who work for you and yours will thrive.

832

No cute messages on your answering machine or voicemail. Ever.

833

There are two ways to build a successful business: by one's own industry, or by the stupidity of one's competition.

834

Don't be foolish and vote for the best president. Vote for the one who will do the least harm.

835

Smart executives know when to join a parade in which they have no interest in order to get where they want to go.

836
Take risks.

837
The wise CEO knows that every great chairman was once a junior executive.

838
Blessed are those who travel in circles,
for they shall be known as wheels.

839
All businesspeople can be reduced to two distinct categories: those who borrow, and those who lend.

840
If all executives thought before they spoke,
the silence would be deafening.

841
The best time to sell a horse is before it dies.

842

Experience is what you get
when you don't get what you want.

843

Inherited wealth has promoted more executives
than hard work.

844

Be careful when you stand up to be counted.
Someone might take your seat.

845

"If two men on the same job agree all the time, then
one is useless. If they disagree all the time, then
both are useless."
– Darryl Zanuck

846

On Wall Street, "ethics" is defined as a set of rules
created by executives to identify how they would
act if their businesses were profitable.

847
Lose Weight.

848
Never check anything irreplaceable on to an airplane.

849
It is not smart to put your name on the first parking space … that should say "Visitor."

850
There's no such thing as a hard sell or a soft sell. There's only the stupid sell and the smart sell.

851
Be a customer. Call your own sales office once a quarter and try to buy something.

852
"It's not the employer who pays the wages. Employers only handle the money. It's the customer who pays the wages."
– Henry Ford

Ben Frankly says ...

"If you keep doing what you're doing,
you'll keep getting what you're getting."

854

Of all of our senses,
common sense is clearly the most important.

855

Some executives are successful because they act successful. Attitude makes a difference.

856

Dumb executives are the ones who expend energy to raise their voice rather than to reinforce their argument.

857

Smart executives don't admire employees for how hard they work ... they admire them for how much they get done.

858

Absence doesn't make the heart grow fonder in business. Speak to your customers often.

859
If you can't break 100,
don't play golf with your boss.

860
"The higher you climb the flagpole,
the more people see your rear end."
– Don Meredith

861
Most executives in the 1980s lived so far beyond
their incomes that they were forced to purchase
BMWs just to keep up.

862
Executives who make themselves into sheep
will probably be eaten by wolves.

863
If everything in business were fair,
the losing lawyer wouldn't get paid.

864

Good planning always costs less than good reacting.

865

Any company with more chiefs than Indians shall be 110% ahead of its competition in meetings.

866

Foolish ideas dressed up to look impressive
are usually dreamed up by impressive fools.

867

Tough times don't last very long …
tough people do.

868

Many corporations encourage independent thinking right up until the day they fire you for it. Don't let yours be one of them.

"Hendrickson has taken corporate golf to a whole new level."

870

"If I had eight hours to chop down a tree
I would spend six hours sharpening my ax."
– Abraham Lincoln

871

Have a wide enough sphere of interests that you don't always talk shop.

872

The most valuable lesson one can learn from going to meetings is that most of them are not necessary.

873

In the 1980s most bankers were so addicted to exaggeration that they couldn't tell the truth without lying.

874

Show me an executive who hasn't fantasized about getting in his car and quitting his job, and I'll show you an executive who doesn't drive.

875

Anyone can pilot a ship in a calm sea.

876

The wise public relations executive is a person who thinks twice before saying nothing.

877

Most CFOs know that if your outgo exceeds your income, your upkeep will be your downfall.

878

"Success is more a function of consistent common sense than it is of genius."

– An Wang
Founder of Wang Computer

879

**TRY TO BE SENSITIVE
TO YOUR CUSTOMERS' NEEDS**

Consider the average drug store ... they make the sick walk all the way to the back of the store to get their prescriptions filled while healthy people can buy their cigarettes up front.

880

Some executives create more enthusiasm when they leave a room than when they enter it.

881

Not everyone can be a hero. Someone has to sit on the curb and clap as the hero marches by.

882

Management seminars are designed to teach executives new ways to make it difficult for people to get any work done.

883

Executives who look good, sound good, and act good will get by in corporate life … even if they're stupid.

884

If you make your employees feel bad, they will wind up only doing the things they think will make you feel good.

885

Always make sure you have what you need
before you begin.

886

Your boss will seldom remember when you are
right and never forget when you are wrong.

887

If you've never made a mistake,
you've never made anything.

888

Watch all your competitors regardless of size.
A small business can become a big problem overnight.

889

It has been said that only stupid lawyers would
actually solve the problem and eliminate your need
to keep paying them. Does that mean you should
only hire stupid lawyers if you want to get
something done?

Ben Frankly says ...

"When you can't convince them,
confuse them."

891
"No one can make you feel inferior
without your consent."
– Eleanor Roosevelt

892
Procrastination is the art of
keeping up with yesterday.

893
Those who have some money think that the most important thing in the world is love. The poor know it's money.

894
The best job for an employee who constantly says, "Because that's the way we've always done it," is with one of your competitors.

895
When you make every sale a good buy for your customer, that customer will become a good customer.

896

An unreasonable price when buying
becomes quite reasonable when selling.

897

Never delegate responsibility without authority.

898

If you think you can get something for nothing in
business, you shouldn't be in business.

899

Keep a dictating machine in your car – it's where
some of your best ideas come to you.

900

An executive's true character is revealed by what he
or she does when no one is watching.

901

A round peg will never fit into a square hole. Get
the right employee for the right job, or you'll have
an unhappy employee and a botched job.

902
Know when to hold.
Know when to fold.

903
Share your success and you will be more likely to repeat it.

904
A good salesperson can drop a feather into the Grand Canyon and have you standing there waiting for the echo.

905
In whatever you say to a customer, consistency is the key. Therefore, it is both easier and wiser to be truthful.

906
The difference between an experienced businessman and an educated businessman is that an educated businessman recognizes his mistakes and then makes them again.

907

YOUR JOB ISN'T OVER UNTIL THE JOB IS DONE

It is almost difficult to imagine that the following story from my book, *A Spirit of Greatness; Stories from the Employees of American Airlines,* actually happened. It exemplifies an exceptional level of job commitment, and human decency, that we seem to be moving away from in our "get it to me yesterday" businessworld:

Carter Bibbey started as an American Airlines agent working the 4 p.m.-to-midnight shift. After the last flight of the day from Los Angeles had arrived a very harried man approached Carter saying that his checked luggage was nowhere to be found. Carter's apology and explanation of AA's lost luggage procedure did nothing to calm the man who frantically explained that he was conducting a training seminar early the next morning and all of his materials were in the lost bag – his job was on the line.

Carter took the passenger's information and after the man had left, he continued with a system-wide search to locate the missing luggage. Carter had no success and as he ended his shift at midnight he was feeling very badly for the desperate passenger. In one last attempt to find the luggage he checked an area in another carrier's baggage room – a long shot.

For some reason the luggage had been incorrectly routed, and there it sat.

Carter grabbed the bags and drove from Boston to Rhode Island to personally deliver the valuable cargo. At 4 a.m. the undoubtedly startled passenger received his presentation materials. Carter later received a "Customer Comes First" watch from American, and American Airlines earned a devoted customer.

"Getting it done" is the key to success in any business. And, just think how good it feels to know that you went the extra distance to improve someone else's life.

908
Lend ... don't borrow.

909
Never encourage your son
to date your boss' daughter.

910
The easiest way to knock a chip off someone's shoulder is to give them a pat on the back.

"I don't think I'll get my wife a Christmas present this year. She still hasn't used the lawnmower I bought her last year."

912

If you are going to lose your job, be sure it's for what you did … not for what you didn't do.

913

In business there are two types of employees: those who work as if they are employees, and those who work as if they are employers. When a promotion becomes available, who do you think will get the position?

914

In business, as in history, you can always identify the pioneer who takes big risks and moves into new territories ... he's the one with all the arrows in his back! But we would have never reached new frontiers without them.

915

In business, as in life, the worst itches are always in spots where you don't want the public to see you scratching.

916
Be the first to say hello.

917
Insist that your employees focus on how to get it done, rather than on why it can't be done.

918
To enjoy success, you've got to experience some failure in your life; otherwise you won't appreciate the difference.

919
"Failure Is Only The Opportunity To Begin Again More Intelligently."
This maxim is credited to Henry Ford, but there are so many other successful people that come to mind every time I read it. One of my most favorite heroes is the legendary Colonel Sanders. In 1952, at the age of 62, while in personal bankruptcy, he started the Kentucky Fried Chicken Company in Corbin, Kentucky. While living out of his car, with only a recipe for fried chicken and a $105-a-month Social Security check, he began again and went on to build a multimillion dollar food company.

920

"There are two primary choices in life: to accept conditions as they exist, or accept the responsibility for changing them."

– Dennis Waitley

Author of *The Psychology of Winning*

IT'S BEEN FOUR HOURS ...
DO YOU KNOW WHERE YOUR FAMILY IS?

CONCLUSION

On a very personal note, I would like to add to my belief that along with the obvious advantages that success in business brings, comes important obligations. One of those obligations is to put back at least some of what we have taken out and do our part to insure the future growth of our business community. That future is directly and proportionately related to the quality of the education we provide for our children. Our country has rapidly moved away from its roots as a manufacturing and industrial society. Business is becoming increasingly technology-reliant and much less restricted by geographical boundaries each year. Workers must become literate in math, computer science, economics, and general business skills to even survive in an entry-level position in today's aggressive, competitive, and profit conscious business community.

The deterioration of the educational system in America, mainly as a result of budget cuts and particularly in our elementary schools, is of great concern. I personally believe the growth in social problems (such as welfare) is directly linked to the decreasing quality of our educational system. Of even greater concern, we now know we have lost the window of motivation for many of our children before they even graduate from high school.

In addition to the vast reductions in quality education, consider that twenty years ago most children in grades K-12 could not find a place to buy drugs, even if they wanted to. Fifteen years ago most children never considered suicide, regardless of the severity of their depression. Ten years ago many mothers were not forced back to work due to economic uncertainty, and at least one parent was always there to prepare dinner and establish a secure home environment with strong family values.

The twentieth century has brought with it changes in attitudes, and motivation, and significant reductions in ethics and moral values that responsible business leaders must react to. The popular focus of these executives with insight has historically been the support of children at the college level.

It is now clear that today our support must be directed to children at a much earlier age, particularly our high-risk, inner-city children who are struggling under depressed economic conditions, pressure to try drugs, rampant criminal dangers, single parent environments, and a significant decline in moral and religious values.

Success in business brings a responsibility to give our children at least the same chance to succeed that we had growing up.

Twenty years ago my friend, Ray Chambers, the founder and chairman of Wesray, made a great impact on me. Ray is one of the largest supporters of high-risk children I know and he opened my eyes to the need for the business community to support education. I joined the board of one of the most prestigious independent schools in New England and have worked very hard to raise funding for a variety of scholarship funds for high-risk children. Several years ago, I took a position on the Organizing Committee of the Presidents' Summit for America's Future. It evolved into an organization called "America's Promise" and it was chaired by General Colin Powell. I am honored to have assisted him.

If this book helps you focus on being more successful in business, I hope it also motivates you to take an active role in some program to help educate our children and, in particular, our high-risk children. They represent the future of our business community.

I wish to particularly thank those executives who shared a small measure of their wisdom with me in this book; my wife for putting up with my endless business activities; my children for having what they call an "eccentric dad"; and my mother, father, and sister for getting me this far.

I hope the maxims and anecdotes in this book help you live your personal and business lives better.

Clearly, they are great for speechwriters and many are great to share with younger employees who will someday be great leaders.